Coming Back

A Guide to Recovering from Heart Attack
and Living Confidently with
Coronary Disease

D1616271

Coming Back

A Guide to Recovering from Heart Attack
and Living Confidently with
Coronary Disease

KEITH COHN, M.D.
DARBY DUKE, R.N.
JOSEPH A. MADRID

Illustrated by
Craig Stilwell

ADDISON-WESLEY PUBLISHING COMPANY

READING, MASSACHUSETTS • MENLO PARK, CALIFORNIA
LONDON • AMSTERDAM • DON MILLS, ONTARIO • SYDNEY

Sponsoring editor: William Burgower
Development, editing, production: Brian Williams
Design: Rick Chafian
Graphic art: Boardworks
Typesetting: Graphic Typesetting Service

Library of Congress Cataloging in Publication Data

Cohn, Keith, 1935-
  Coming back.

  Bibliography: p.
  Includes index.
  1. Heart—Infarction—Prevention. 2. Cardiovascular
patient—Rehabilitation. 3. Coronary heart disease—Prevention.
I. Duke, Darby, 1949-   joint author. II. Madrid, Joseph A.,
1924-   joint author. III. Title. [DNLM: 1. Coronary
disease—Rehabilitation—Popular works. WG113 C678c]
RC685.I6C63   616.1'23   78-60826
ISBN 0-201-04561-3

The authors and publishers have exerted every effort to insure that drug selec-
tion and dosage set forth in this text are in accord with current recommendations and practice at the time of publication. However, in view of ongoing research, changes in government regulations and the constant flow of information relating to drug therapy and drug reactions, the reader is urged to check
the package insert for each drug for any change in indications of dosage and
for added warnings and precautions. This is particularly important where the
recommended agent is a new and/or infrequently employed drug.

ISBN 0-201-04561-3 P
ISBN 0-201-04562-1 H
ABCDEFGHIJ-DO-79

To Buddy Langston, our colleague and friend,
who cared and loved
and
lived life abundantly

CONTENTS

FOREWORD

Norman E. Shumway, M.D.
Professor of Cardiovascular Surgery
Stanford University School of Medicine

ONE of the most difficult tasks for the physician is that of stating clearly and concisely to the heart patient in lay language just what is happening to him or her. Yet this task is important, since fear of the unknown—or rather fear of not knowing—is frequently more devastating to the patient than the medical setback itself is. *Coming Back* is a precise and comprehensible book that touches on all aspects of what the coronary patient wants and needs to know.

The authors nicely analyze the kinds of care, the hospital stay, the posthospital convalescence—including the all-important rehabilitation period—and even the seemingly complicated electronic equipment. In addition, because there has been so much emphasis on coronary bypass surgery, both in the lay press and in medical journals, the authors wisely stress the many other, nonsurgical approaches that offer comparable recovery results. Contrary to popular opinion, certainly not every patient with coronary artery disease is a candidate for surgery.

The dominant theme of this book is how to cope intelligently and effectively with a heart attack if it surfaces unexpectedly or prematurely. But there are lessons here as well for the reader who has not yet suffered a heart attack. If you live long enough, you will generally manifest some deterioration of your cardiovascular system. *Coming Back* shows you how to postpone or prevent that occurrence as effectively as possible.

INTRODUCTION

What This Book Is About

A heart attack is a frightening event that afflicts nearly one and a half million Americans every year. In addition, several million others develop some form of coronary disease. It's evident we face a problem of epidemic proportions.

But what is often overlooked is that a vast number of people who have suffered heart or coronary damage make a complete or nearly complete recovery and resume healthy, active, busy lives. Presidents Dwight D. Eisenhower and Lyndon B. Johnson, for instance, suffered heart attacks and still were able to continue their political careers. Many other famous figures in entertainment, business, the sciences, and the arts have also bounced back—some from bouts of coronary pain, others from full-fledged heart attacks.

Such people made their comebacks not only because of good medical care—good monitoring, drug administration, and other therapy—but, most importantly, because they decided to take care of themselves.

Coming Back describes the first part of the process, explaining what goes on in the hospital, what certain drugs do, and other hospital-related things. But it is mainly concerned with the second part—helping you get back on your feet once you're back at home. It shows how you can overcome lingering fears and anxieties and help yourself back to a normal life or as nearly a normal life as circumstances permit.

And if you've been fortunate enough not to have any coronary problems in the first place, *Coming Back* shows you how they may be avoided.

The book has thus been written with the following points in mind:

- The information is presented from the *patient's viewpoint,* not the doctor's or nurse's. It is therefore expressed in layman's terms. At the same time, extensive additional information is offered in the back of the book which may be of interest to those who want to know more (see "Further Explorations").

- The information is presented like a *smorgasbord or salad bar.* You don't have to help yourself to everything. Feel free to skip the chapters that don't seem to apply to you. (If you don't smoke or drink, for example, or don't have chest pains or heart-rhythm disturbances, then you really don't care about them, and it's O.K. to skip those parts.)

- The information is presented in clear, *bite-sized, easily digestible* chunks. All chapters are short—usually only a few pages each.

- The information is presented in as *interesting and lively* a manner as is possible. Why should a helpful book be a dull book? We have tried to write this in a warm, personal, sympathetic, and above all interesting style. We have tried to encourage your involvement and awareness by providing self-diagnostic questionnaires, diagrams by which you can compare yourself to others, charts showing the odds for different kinds of health risks, and illustrations that clearly explain medical concepts and principles yet avoid a heavy medical and anatomical look unless absolutely required to make a point understandable.

• The information is *practical and current*. When we did not feel information was useful, we did not put it in. When it seemed to be a subject people were interested in (we get a lot of questions about coronary bypass, for instance—even from people who probably would not be candidates for the procedure), we gave it the space it deserved. The book is filled with useful tips to help you deal with threatening feelings and murky emotions, learn how to quit smoking, change your eating habits so meals become *more* rather than less interesting, and much more.

Although the book principally is intended for heart and coronary patients, many may want their families and friends to read it—if only to avoid what they themselves have suffered.

Ready to start your comeback? Turn the page.

CHAPTER 1

Like a Bolt from the Blue:
Days 1 – 3

Pᴇʀʜᴀᴘs it began as a burning, constricted feeling, a dull or heavy pain—the worst pain you have ever felt. Or perhaps it was simply a vague ache or discomfort, virtually unnoticed, even not noticed at all. Perhaps you thought you had indigestion, and even your doctor may have had difficulty telling that it was not simply an overdose of lasagna at dinner. Or perhaps you suddenly felt very weak, began sweating profusely, experienced a sense of impending doom, indeed, actually passed out.

There are many ways a heart attack can occur. It may have happened while you were sleeping, eating, driving, or at work. Like a bolt from the blue, it may have happened suddenly, without warning, at any time of day or night. On the other hand, it may have been preceded by hours, days, or even weeks of vague chest pains or general feelings of not-so-well-being. It may have been preceded by some exertion—gardening, lifting, playing tennis, even making love—or it may not. It may have been precipitated by emotional stress—conflict with your boss, an argument with another driver, great upset in the family—or it may not. Indeed, a heart attack is often preceded by *no* exertion or provocation whatsoever.

Doctors would prefer that there be as little time as possible between the onset of a heart attack and entry into the hospital, but it seldom happens that quickly. While people around you may have thought you looked ill—sweaty, pallid—you may have insisted you were O.K., maybe argued about what should be done, finally agreed to take an aspirin or Alka-Seltzer or lie down for a nap. Finally, someone called a doctor or the hospital and, perhaps after further debate about how to get you there (drive yourself? call an ambulance?), one way or another you wound up in the emergency room.

Then things probably began to happen very rapidly. The nurse or physician, suspecting a possible heart attack, ordered you onto a gurney or bed. Intravenous fluids were started in your arm. Blood samples were drawn. An electrocardiogram was taken. Wires were attached to your chest and connected to a monitoring device. Perhaps a chest x-ray was taken. Physicians and nurses probed with hands and listened with stethoscopes and asked a great many questions: How did you feel? What did you eat? Where, exactly, was the pain?

Then there came the decision whether or not to hospitalize you, and the physician confronted you and your family with the matter. Again, you may have protested that you were "basically O.K.," that you had a lot of things to do and had to get home, and you may have felt angry toward the hospital staff and your family for insisting that you were sick.

At about this point, however, you may also have begun to realize the enormity of the situation, a concern that became magnified when you began thinking back to the real world: Relatives would have to be called, the boss or subordinates notified, scheduled events cancelled. A thousand fears, worries, and questions may have surfaced. Will I be disabled, an invalid? Will I die? Will I be able to work, play, have sex, lead a normal life again? All the while, confusion reigned, because the amount of information being given you was either too little or so profuse that you would have had difficulty following it even if you weren't being given sedatives.

Finally, you were transferred to the coronary care unit (CCU) or similar intensive-care facility. There you were surrounded by an array of uncommon-looking, even frightening, electronic devices. Again, wires were placed on your chest and connected to a monitoring instrument at the central nursing station, where nurses continuously monitored your heart's electrical activity and heartbeat, as well as, perhaps, your blood pressure and respiration rate. You may have received oxygen through small nasal tubes. Periodically you were given intravenous solutions as well as medicines for everything from sleeping to heart-rhythm stabilization.

During this time you may actually have felt perfectly well. You had had your episode of chest pain and it disappeared and you just wanted to get out of there and go home. On the other hand, you may have experienced recurring bouts of chest pain, weakness, shortness of breath, or irregular heart rhythm. Thus, you may either have found yourself in a quiet room—waiting for something to happen, introspective, contemplative—or you may have found yourself critically ill, with a flurry of activity about you from time to time.

Of course your normal living habits were affected. Because of the diet prescribed by your physician, your meals—meager, semiliquid, salt-restricted—varied greatly from what you were used to. Depending on the severity of your heart attack, you may have found yourself restrained by your physician from doing your usual activities: not allowed to get out of bed, wash, shave, sit in a chair, even go to the bathroom (instead forced to use a bedside commode). Exercise, if any, probably consisted of a nurse or physical therapist helping you with simple arm and leg movements. These alterations in your normal activities you probably found demeaning and confusing, if not indeed frightening.

All of the above describe the first two or three days following a heart attack. If you are at this point, you and your family are confronted with one of the most important events in your lives, with many implications, both immediate and long-term. At the moment you may feel a tremendous sense of helplessness, like a hostage trapped in the coronary care unit, required to follow restrictions and instructions, some of them uncomfortable, some of which you may disagree with, many of which make little sense. Even if you have not been through such a traumatic experience—if, for instance, you are suffering from angina, the chest pains of coronary disease, or if you have had a bypass operation—that can still be very unsettling, and you may have many worries and doubts about the future.

However, most heart patients eventually come through the hospitalization with little difficulty. Many make a comeback to a completely or nearly completely active, productive, exciting life—often more enjoyable than the one they had before.

And that's what this book is about: coming back.

CHAPTER 2

In the Hospital: What's Going On Around Here?

If you are still in the coronary care unit (CCU) or elsewhere in the hospital, this chapter may help you understand what's going on—who those people are that are checking your progress, what instruments they are working with, what the hospital routine is about. (If you have been discharged from the hospital, you may want to skip this chapter and move on to Chapter 3.)

Let's start with the people.

Medical Personnel

The attending physician may be your family doctor, an internist, or a cardiologist (or all three). His or her job is to act as the quarterback for the medical team, to diagnose and treat your condition and counsel you and your family.

The coronary care unit nurse, a nurse who specializes in the care of heart disease, constantly watches patients when they are first admitted to the hospital,

monitors the vital signs, administers any medication or therapy prescribed by the physician, watches for adverse psychological reactions and tries to help alleviate them, and in other ways is the heart patient's primary contact with all the medical specialists involved. You should consider the nurse, whether in the CCU or elsewhere, a valuable immediate and primary resource, both in the early, unsure beginning and later on, when you've returned home and may need to telephone for advice.

Other members of the recovery team are the physical therapist, dietitian, occupational therapist, and psychological counselor or clergyman, although not all of these specialists are present in all hospitals.

The physical therapist is an expert in body movements and exercise, and will show you how to exercise for maximum benefit without straining the heart and blood vessels.

The dietitian can explain what eating habits may have contributed to—and could aggravate further—the heart disease, and can develop menus of safe foods for you.

The occupational therapist can show you how to cope with activities after your release—how to bathe, cook, garden, and so on, in ways that pose the least stress for your heart and cardiovascular system.

A psychological counselor—psychologist, psychiatrist, minister, priest, rabbi—can help you cope with the fears, doubts, and anxieties that inevitably follow a heart attack. Don't hesitate to call on any of these people for advice.

In many hospitals the doctor and nurse will assist you in these various areas.

Equipment and Instruments

The coronary care unit (or similar intensive-care facility) is designed to allow maximum patient observation and care. However, the specialized electronic monitoring devices, which are usually located near your bed, can be intimidating indeed. The purpose of these devices is to relay moment-to-moment information about the electrical activity of your heart to the central nursing station, where it is under constant surveillance by the nursing staff. This information is available as it is happening, but the central nursing station equipment also has a memory capability, so that the staff can compare how your heart is operating now with how it was operating a few minutes ago.

Here are what the various instruments in the CCU do:

ELECTROCARDIOGRAM.   When your doctor wants to print out a complete record of your heart's electrical activity and rhythm, an electrocardiographic machine is often wheeled into your room. This records the heart's electrical activity on graph paper. The electrocardiograms (also called ECG or EKG) tell how fast the heart is beating and whether there are any irregularities in the heart rhythm. Electrocardiograms are taken when you are first admitted to the hospital and for two or more days afterwards, since changes in the electrical patterns help prove whether or not a heart attack did indeed take place.

It might be of interest for you to know that, even after the heart is completely healed from an attack, in the subsequent months or years to come, the ECG often continues to show a permanent sign, an imprint, of the previous heart attack, and this record can be used to help doctors keep an eye on your heart in the future.

THE OSCILLOSCOPE.   A slightly different kind of electrocardiogram can be used for continuous *monitoring* surveillance of the moment-to-moment changes in the rhythm of the heart. Small discs called electrodes are stuck to your chest and are attached by wires to devices called oscilloscopes, one of which is usually located in your room

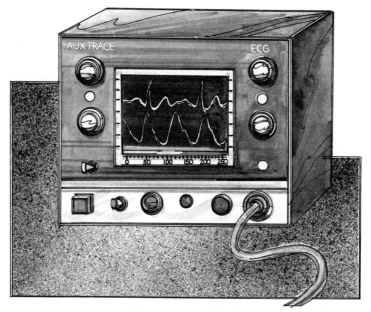

Heart monitor

and another at the central nursing station. The oscilloscope is like the screen of a television set, only it shows wavelike lines, which represent the electricity of your heart. This electrical information is relayed to the central nursing station, where doctors and nurses can immediately see what is happening and be alerted to any unusual or unexpected changes in the behavior in the heart.

TELEMETRY. Some monitoring systems are not connected to the oscilloscopes by wires. Rather, electrodes attached to your chest relay ECG signals to the central nursing station via radio transmission. This telemetry is used not only in some coronary care units but also sometimes for patients moved to less intensive care setting. Telemetry permits you to move about more freely, since you are not constrained by wires, and the medical staff can watch your reactions while you walk around the room or ward.

MONITORING OF PRESSURES WITHIN THE HEART.   In most cases, your blood pressure is taken using the typical arm cuff and stethoscope. In some heart attacks, however, the blood pressure, and other pressures within the heart and lungs, can be watched by means of a small tube inserted into the arteries and veins. It is even possible to "float" a thin tube through the veins and heart into the lungs to record pressures there. Such devices are usually reserved for patients who require more intensive monitoring, and they may be helpful in deciding whether any change in therapy need be initiated.

TELEVISION MONITORS.   In some hospitals, if you are in a room out of sight of the nursing staff, a TV camera transmits a closed-circuit picture to the central nursing station, so the nurses have a clear view of you at all times.

INTRAVENOUS FEEDING.   Most patients in the coronary care unit are given a small needle or tube in their vein so that the doctor or nurse may give medication at a moment's notice. In many cases, a glass bottle or plastic bag is attached to the needle with clear plastic tubing, so that you can be fed with sugar water or provided with a constant "drip" of medicines, if needed.

So much for instruments and equipment. What about the hospital regimen?

Hospital Activities

We will not get into medication and diet here; they are covered in later chapters. (Some of these medications are explained in Chapters 7 through 10 and also in Appendix A. Diet is described in Chapters 15 and 16 and Appendixes B through G.) However, we would like to talk a little about exercise. Surprised? Yes, it starts in the hospital.

In many places, you get exercise while you are still in bed in the CCU or intensive-care unit. A nurse or physical therapist may raise the head of your bed so that you are nearly sitting up, then move your hands up and down in circular motions in the air and flex your legs, wrists, and ankles. This activity is called *passive range-of-motion exercising,* because someone other than you is providing the energy for the movement. By the second or third day of your convalescence, perhaps, you'll be asked to perform these exercises by yourself *(active range-of-motion exercises)*. At about this time also, you will be encouraged to wash your own face and hands and brush your teeth, and you will be allowed some TV watching and light reading.

After a while, you will be allowed to do the range-of-motion exercises sitting in a chair. You may feel faint at first, owing to a temporary drop in blood pressure caused by your going from complete bed rest to the more demanding activity in a chair. However, this will go away as you begin to move about and become more active. Of course, the degree of activity and length of time devoted to exercise will vary from patient to patient, depending on the severity of the heart attack.

After you have been transferred out of the CCU to a regular hospital room or ward, you will be asked to do your exercises in a standing position. Later, you will be asked to walk about in your room or the hospital halls, and you will probably be expected to count your own pulse carefully. At the same time, you will advance from taking sponge baths to taking tub baths or showers, using standard toilet facilities, and to playing cards or other games.

In the few days prior to your discharge from the hospital, the nurse or physical therapist may assist you in climbing stairs, beginning with three or four steps and progressing to short flights.

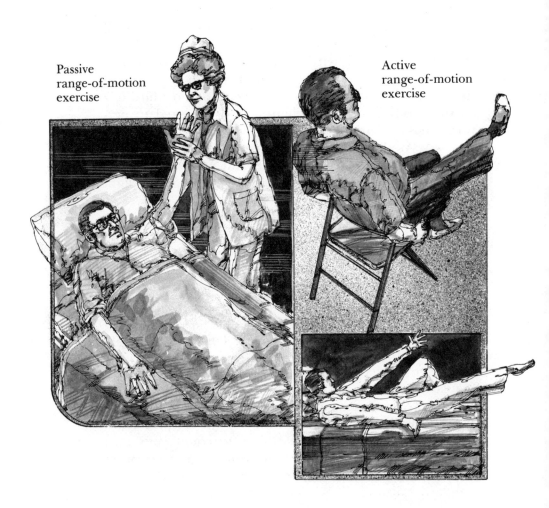

Passive
range-of-motion
exercise

Active
range-of-motion
exercise

A Word about Doctor's Orders

We see two rather interesting phenomena among patients: Some make nervous wrecks of themselves and their families (and their physicians) by charging into their recovery and compulsively trying to follow everything the doctor says to the letter. Others simply ignore everything the doctor says and, for example, overexert themselves or fail to take their medications. Neither kind of behavior is desirable.

The thing to understand is the difference between orders and advice.

In general, *advice* is what your physician recommends about such things as diet and exercise. It is just that—advice—and that means modifications can be made. (Of course you don't have to stick to your diet on your birthday.)

Orders, on the other hand, apply to medications (and anything else the doctor particularly emphasizes). It is important not to miss medications, switch them around, change doses, or in other ways tamper with the program since otherwise they not only might not work but might actually be harmful.

End of speech.

The Future

While in the hospital you will probably be getting a lot of instructions and advice about medication, diet, and so on, which you are supposed to follow once you get home. The rest of this book is intended to assist in that, so that during the forthcoming weeks and months, you can get back to the best state of health possible.

However, simply having this book in your possession will do nothing for you. It must be read, perhaps more than once, until you know the information is working for you. *You and your participation* are the key to your recovery.

CHAPTER 3

Feelings: Frustrations, Gripes, Tensions, Blues

JOHN Abbott, 55, a heavy-equipment operator, suffered a heart attack but recovered uneventfully. In the hospital his physician advised him to follow a low-cholesterol diet, to stop smoking, to avoid emotional stress, to eliminate heavy work temporarily, and to undertake a progressive physical exercise program. Shortly after his admission to the hospital, his chest pains disappeared and he had no additional symptoms. Thereupon he repeatedly demanded to be released, insisting that he hadn't had a heart attack but only some stomach disorder and heartburn. Four days after his discharge from the hospital, Abbott (not his real name) was discovered by his wife trying to move a heavy couch in the living room. He was also smoking a cigarette. A heated argument followed, and Abbott stomped angrily out of the house, leaving his wife confused and in tears.

Louis Meehan (also not his real name), 37, had only recently been promoted to vice-president in a metropolitan bank, when he suffered a heart attack accompanied by severe chest pain. He, too, recovered uneventfully, but weeks after his release from the hospital, when he should have been functioning almost normally, he continued to lack energy, was tired much of the time, felt low and discouraged, and had little motivation toward both his job and his previous interests. Formerly a talkative, outgoing person, he became quiet and withdrawn and oftentimes just sat around sadly and moped.

Until her heart attack, Eva Steinfield, 45, had been an active housewife, caring for three children as well as holding down a part-time job. Four months after leaving the hospital, however, she was unable to keep up with shopping and cleaning, had to beg out of her share of the car pool, and relied more and more on her husband to cope with the household and make decisions about the kids. Moreover, her life virtually centered around telephone calls and office visits to her physician, to whom she expressed concerns about a variety of aches and pains and repeatedly asked him about her medicines, potential remedies she had read about in magazines, and so on.

Are these patients being "unrealistic"? Perhaps. But their responses are extremely common. Nearly everyone who has a heart attack appears to develop some emotional problem, and although changes in personality or manner may seem eccentric, they are not hard to understand, considering the stressful circumstances. Indeed, they can be viewed as being the *reasonable results* of one's having to face a life-threatening experience. Often some outside assistance—from a physician, nurse, psychologist, clergyman, or relative—is required to help with the adjustment.

The thing to understand is that millions of others who have had a heart attack have reacted in similar ways, but, generally speaking, with time and guidance, have outgrown these reactions.

In the CCU

If you were hospitalized for a heart attack in the coronary care unit (CCU), probably your first reaction was one of disbelief. Is this really happening to *me?* The shock of feeling fine one moment and finding yourself in a hospital bed the next, connected to heart telemetry and electrocardiogram wires, is overwhelming. It is an altogether unreal experience, especially if there was no warning. With some patients, this feeling is even expressed briefly as outrage at the fact that blind fate has singled them out for this personal tragedy, and they lash out at their families and the hospital staff.

In the next few hours or days, disbelief gave way to anxiety. You recalled friends and acquaintances who had had heart attacks. Had you considered them "washed up"? Did you wonder if you were washed up yourself? What about the job? Would there be money problems? Would your role in the family change? Would you be able to have sex again? What *does* the future hold?

Even if you were feeling O.K., you might have found yourself just waiting around for some disaster to happen—which, of course, simply added to the anxiety. Thus, you may have become intensely interested in your surroundings, closely observing every movement in the CCU, perhaps staring for hours at the screen of the telemetry unit monitoring your heart. Or you may have had difficulty concentrating, became easily distressed, and found it hard to remember or comprehend instructions (a good reason for hanging on to this book, so that you can review the things you were told and have forgotten).

Many patients at this stage experience talkativeness—probably as a way of releasing nervous tension—as well as restlessness, sleeplessness, sweating, or trembling. By the end of the first week in the hospital, you may have felt completely discouraged and depressed, worried about your future, perhaps even panicky.

If, as you read this, you are still in the hospital, you should try not to let these anxieties overwhelm you and create mischief later on. Talk over your feelings and fears with the hospital staff. That's what they're there for.

Coming Home

What is it like after you have been discharged from the hospital? At the very least you may be troubled by a number of minor complaints: strange aches and pains, sleeplessness, fatigue. These symptoms may seem to crop up all the time, and, of course, the more they occur the worse you feel, and you and your family may become convinced that a disaster lurks around every corner.

What is really happening, however, is merely increased awareness. You have become more concerned with and introspective about yourself and your body, so that you notice every little ache and pain, even though your physician might already have judged them insignificant. As for the fatigue, you may have less zip merely because you have been inactive for awhile and have not yet started an exercise program.

Most of these kinds of complaints will probably begin to disappear as time goes by. The best attitude to take is to understand that they do occur, discuss them with your physician so he or she can evaluate their significance, then deliberately put yourself in a positive frame of mind, in effect "shaking off" those minor complaints.

What about the *major* complaints, the larger emotions? How are you handling the fact that you had a heart attack? That depends on the kind of person you are, for, as we saw with the examples at the beginning of this chapter, people handle stress in different ways. Following the numbing shock that occurs during the first few days, the disbelief and anger, you probably reacted to the event in one of four ways:

- You continued to have strong feelings of *anxiety,* dwelling—perhaps obsessively—on the potential future danger of your illness.

- You may have become moderately to seriously *depressed,* as banker Louis Meehan did. Perhaps you became more quiet and withdrawn, your movements became slower and less bouncy, you lost some appetite, lost interest in your job or other major hobbies, or experienced vague feelings of fatigue, discouragement, sadness, or anxiety, even began weeping. Indeed, you may have become unwilling to venture far from home, becoming absorbed in your own despondency to the exclusion of all other interests.

- Like John Abbott, you may have actually *denied* you really had an illness—simply did not accept that such a fearful thing had happened, ignored pleas to give up smoking, lose weight, keep regular doctor's appointments. Indeed, some people, believing the heart attack beyond their control, respond by simply rejecting it, not acknowledging that anything serious has happened, contesting the diagnosis, minimizing the extent of the illness, and disregarding any restrictions.

- Like Mrs. Steinfield, you may have become exceedingly *dependent* on your physician, family, and friends. Some patients may even tend to revere the physician as a godlike figure and to become extraordinarily dependent on everyone for emotional sustenance and physical assistance.

Anxiety, depression, denial, dependency. Any one or a combination of these can occur.

And they often develop in the first month or so after a heart attack.

Acceptance

In all the welter of conflicting emotions, *acceptance* may be
the hardest, but it is the one that gives you the best
chance of returning to a normal life. Why you had a
heart attack isn't always easy to explain, but the fact remains that you *did* and you *are* temporarily disabled.

When you return home from the hospital, you will
be confined to some extent for at least 2 to 3 weeks. You
may reexperience some of the feelings you had immediately after your heart attack, and you may thus find
yourself irritated by the restrictions, the limited physical
area, the sounds of children squabbling, the lack of things
to do. You may find that an oversolicitous spouse can
make the adjustment difficult. You may be worried about
curtailments in your income. You may wonder if you can
get back to a normal sex life. How do you handle all of
these problems?

In dealing with your family and spouse, it is important that all of you recognize the apprehensions everyone
has and that these anxieties be talked about openly. Good
communications and free expression of real feelings will
tend to lessen fears and prevent angry outbursts. Group
sessions, in which several families share common experi-
ences, may also represent a valuable way to uncover vex-
ing problems. Ask your physician or nurse for recommendations.

Money worries can be a real cause of anxiety. The
important thing to appreciate is that the faster you regain
your health, the sooner you may be able to return to
work. With your acceptance of your disability and your
willingness to participate in your own recovery, this will
happen sooner, not later.

Similarly with sex: Heart disease does not impair
sexual function. Patients who have suffered heart attacks
are just as capable of having healthy and satisfying sex

lives as they were before. After all, it was the heart that was affected by your attack, not the rest of the body.

What if your physician says that your heart attack was a serious one, that there is a possibility that you may not reach full recovery? We don't want to raise false fears here, but some patients with extremely severe angina or very severe congestive heart failure are limited to various extents and cannot return to a normal life. There are varying degrees of incapacity and disability, which determine the extent to which one can return to work and to full-time recreational activities. But there is no sense sitting around worrying about these possibilities. You should simply decide you're going to try and do the best you can to return to as full and active a life as possible.

Keeping yourself occupied with a positive attitude goes a long way toward minimizing most of these problems. (Avoid repeated use of tranquilizers and too much booze—they're no way to cope over the long haul.) Remember: *the life expectancy of most people who survive a heart attack is better than most people think,* and most people who have had an attack go on to lead their lives as before.

The secret is in (1) acceptance and (2) a positive approach to coming back.

CHAPTER **4**

For the Spouse, Family, and Friends

I<small>N</small> the 14 days her husband was in the hospital for a mild heart attack, Sylvia Adams (a pseudonym, as are the others in this chapter) practically camped out at his bedside and kept copious notes on everything the staff members said. Later, when he had returned home, she insisted he follow every aspect of his come-back program to the letter. She threw out every high-calorie, high-cholesterol food item in the house; stopped buying ice cream, Mr. Adams's favorite food; and harangued him when he ordered it in a restaurant.

She kept careful track of his medications (he took eight pills a day) and followed him around with a glass of water until he took each one. She timed his exercises with a stopwatch and even tried to take his pulse. Every Friday she insisted they participate in a group discussion with other heart-attack couples—basically a good idea, but the time conflicted with his weekly poker game.

In short, Mrs. Adams followed Mr. Adams's recovery program very well. Mr. Adams found her attentions a damned nuisance and resented being watched all the time.

What should be a physician's advice here? It should be to Mrs. Adams: "Relax. It is unnecessary to follow each instruction *precisely.* The suggestions being made are simply prudent ones that should be followed the majority of the time."

In other words, although the doctor's instructions about *medications* should be followed exactly, the other advice—about diet, exercise, and the like—can be given greater latitude.

A second case: When his wife suffered a serious heart attack that hospitalized her for 6 weeks, Hugh Carlson, 55, was devastated. They had been married for 34 years and she had never been ill. She had stood with him through lean, rocky years and only recently had they finally had the time and money to enjoy themselves. When he came to see her in the hospital, he paced the floor and was unable to relax and visit. At home he didn't eat and sat for hours with the light off, doing nothing.

When Mrs. Carlson came home to a program of rest and slow recovery, he sat by her bed, holding her hand and fidgeting and talking very little. He showed little interest in his business and left all decisions to his son. He refused to discuss the future, even the next day's events. When the public-health nurse stopped by to check his wife's progress, he was staring out the window. Mrs. Carlson was in tears because she was unable to talk things over with him and felt she could not make any progress without his assistance and support.

What could the nurse have told him? It could be something like: "Look, you're in this together. Offer understanding, sympathy, emotional support; be a listening post; offer some physical assistance. Don't dump a lot of sadness on her. And if you can't shake off that despondency, you should probably seek professional advice."

A third case: Mr. and Mrs. James Newcomb had been married for 27 years, and in all that time he never discussed any health problems with her. When he suffered a moderately severe heart attack, he became angry when she suggested he seek medical assistance. Then, when he was finally hospitalized, he would not permit her to discuss anything with his doctor or nurse. She was not informed of any part of his come-back program, not even what medications he was taking. Because he had a number of heart irregularities and a very slow heart rate, a permanent pacemaker was implanted in him, and after one month he was sent home.

After a while he began having a recurrence of angina. His wife could tell by his facial expressions, nervousness, and general physical appearance that he was now having chest pains, but he denied it vigorously when she asked about it. Indeed, one night he awoke in great distress and asked his wife to get his nitroglycerin for him, but when she asked about it the next morning he laughed and said, "You must have been dreaming."

Mrs. Newcomb knows her husband is a very proud man who doesn't want to admit his weaknesses or burden her with his problems. However, she would like to be informed of his health status and take part in dealing with his problems and planning for further solution. The problem is she doesn't know exactly how to approach him about her wishes. What should we tell her? We'll try to answer this in a minute.

Working as Partners

As the three examples make clear, a heart attack affects not only the patient but his or her partner, as well as close family and friends. How should they handle the change in roles, the change in household and work patterns, the complex emotional reactions (both the patient's and their own)?

In general, we offer four pieces of advice:

- Let the heart-attack patient know that *you* are important, too. How you and the patient interact has a significant effect on the quality of *both* your lives. It's not
just a one-way street.

- Open communication is very important. You must have
a free and honest relationship that encourages expression and venting of emotions, even adverse feelings.
Listen to what the other is saying. Try to understand
what is being said from the other person's point of view
as well as your own. Avoid constant argument, tension,
hostility (read Chapter 3 about the patient's feelings).
Emphasize the positive while still being aware of any
negative feelings.

- Be aware of whatever the plan is for recovery or plans
for the future. These plans should be realistic and
something that you can work on together. Be available
to give assistance when needed and supportive of the
things that you cannot help with.

- Seek guidance, if necessary. Certainly the Adamses,
Carlsons, and Newcombs could have benefited with
professional help in dealing with their relationships. It
is best if both partners or parties agree to this, of
course, but by all means get help for yourself if you feel
you need it—that would be the kind of advice we would
give Mrs. Newcomb, since she was unable to communi-
cate with her balky husband. Discuss any difficulties
with the patient's physician, if he or she is someone you
can talk with, or the nurse in the coronary care unit or
regular ward, or a marriage counselor or a clergyman.
In this connection, you may find so-called "heart clubs"
of value—see Chapter 23.

Facing the Future

Mrs. Ellis, 65, suffered a large heart attack shortly after she and her husband returned from a cross-country trip, and her doctor advised them to cancel their long-planned trip to Europe to visit a daughter and son-in-law. Mr. Ellis had recently retired and was enjoying his free time, and both had been looking forward to doing a good deal more traveling than they had been able to do in the past. The heart attack was, of course, a shock and tremendous disappointment to both of them, and they realized many of their plans would have to change. However, because they cared about each other and were open with each other, they were able to discuss their feelings and make realistic yet satisfactory plans for the future, postponing the trip for a few months.

In short, we cannot emphasize enough the importance of loving concern, open communication, and realistic planning for the future.

CHAPTER **5**

How the Heart Works:
A Crash Course

IN order to understand your particular heart condition and what you can do about it, it is necessary to have an idea about what the heart looks like and how it works. Briefly defined, the heart is a *pump*—a hollow, muscular organ located slightly to the left of center in your chest—which pumps blood through a series of tubes, blood vessels, to provide oxygen and nourishment to the tissues in the body.

How the Heart Is Built

As the illustration on the next page shows, the heart is divided into two sides, left and right. Each side has a lower chamber called a *ventricle*, which pumps the blood out of the heart, and an upper chamber called an *atrium*, which receives the blood returned to the heart.

The walls of the heart are made up of muscle called the *myocardium*, but this muscle is not the same thickness everywhere. The myocardium of the upper chambers (atria) is quite thin compared with the myocardium of the

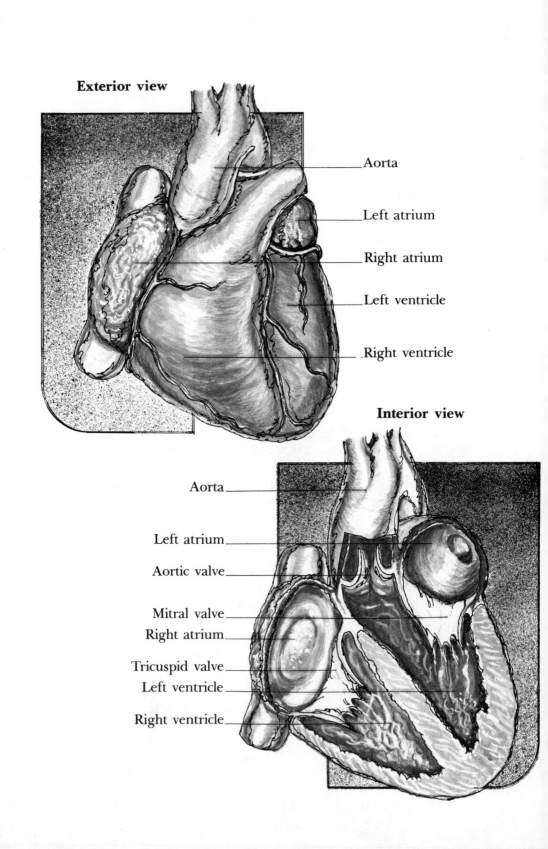

Exterior view

Aorta

Left atrium

Right atrium

Left ventricle

.Right ventricle

Interior view

Aorta

Left atrium

Aortic valve

Mitral valve

Right atrium

Tricuspid valve

Left ventricle

Right ventricle

lower chambers (ventricles). The muscular wall of the left ventricle is three times thicker than that of the right. This powerful left ventricular muscle is often referred to as the "main pump" because, like milking a cow's udder, it squeezes the blood out of the heart to *all* parts of the body with every heartbeat. The heart fills with blood when it is resting (in *diastole*) and pumps the blood out during the contraction (in *systole).*

The upper and lower chambers of the heart are separated by two valves, called *atrioventricular* (AV) *valves.* The left one is called the *mitral* valve, the right, the *tricuspid.* These valves prevent blood from flowing back into the atria from the ventricles when the heart is beating.

Two other valves, called *semilunar valves,* separate the ventricles from the blood vessels that lead from the heart to the lungs and the rest of the body. The left valve is

Diastole   Systole

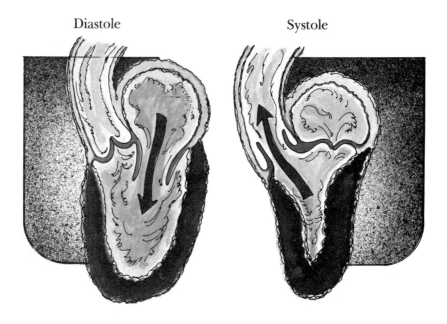

called the *aortic,* and the right valve is called the *pulmonary.* Their function is to prevent the return of blood from the aorta or the pulmonary artery to the ventricles when the heart is resting between beats.

The closing of these valves as the heart beats—first the AV valves, then the semilunar—produces the "lub-dub" sounds a doctor hears when listening through a stethoscope placed on your chest. If the valves are faulty and do not close properly, he or she may hear a "murmur" as the blood leaks backward through these valves.

Go with the Flow

As the illustration opposite shows, the right side of the heart receives blood from all parts of the body. Blood is bright red when it is full of oxygen, but after it returns from the body to the heart, having nourished the tissues and given up a portion of its oxygen, the blood looks slightly bluish or purplish. This incoming blood flows into the right atrium (1 in the drawing), then through the tricuspid valve (2) and into the right ventricle (3), which, on the next contraction or heartbeat, squeezes the blood through the semilunar pulmonary valve (4) through the pulmonary artery (5) into the lungs, which replenish the blood with oxygen.

This oxygen-rich red blood then flows back through the pulmonary veins (6) into the left atrium (7) and through the mitral valve (8) into the left ventricle (9). At the next heartbeat, this left ventricle forcibly contracts its muscular walls and pushes the blood through the aortic valve (10) and out through the aorta (11) to the rest of the body.

How does the blood manage to get to and nourish the tissues? As the illustration shows, the oxygen-rich blood leaves the heart and travels to the tissues of the body through a system of blood vessels, hollow tubes

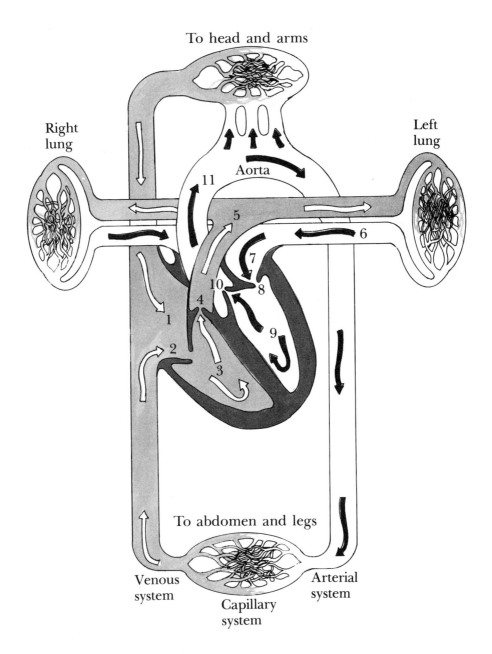

To head and arms

Right
lung

Left
lung

11

Aorta

Right
lung

5

6

7

10
8

4

9

1

2

3

To abdomen and legs

Venous
system

Arterial
system

Capillary
system

The circulatory system

called *arteries.* The aorta is the largest artery, and it divides into smaller arteries, which themselves divide into even smaller arteries—a system much like the limbs, branches, and twigs of a tree.

The smallest arteries empty into one end of a profuse network of tiny blood vessels called *capillaries,* which deliver to the tissues the oxygen and other nutritional substances that the body uses for fuel and energy. These capillaries supply the head, arms, legs and various organs in the abdomen, such as the liver and stomach—and, of course, the heart (the heart in effect feeds itself).

The other end of the capillary network joins with the *veins,* which carry the oxygen-depleted blood back to the heart. The veins are initially small and become larger and larger until they all unite into the largest veins, called the *vena cavae,* which empty into the right atrium of the heart. This brings us full circle.

The heart, arteries, veins, and capillaries are collectively termed the *cardiovascular system.* This amazing circuit assures the adequate delivery of nutritional substances to all the body tissues.

The Heart's Own Arteries

The heart has its own system of arteries called *coronary arteries,* which serve to nourish the heart muscle (myocardium), so that the heart can continue to function as a nonstop pump. These major coronary arteries branch off the aorta, as the third illustration shows, cross over the outside of the heart wall, and penetrate the muscle itself, dividing repeatedly into smaller and smaller branches. The left main coronary artery divides into the left anterior descending artery, which supplies the front, and the circumflex, which goes to the left side and around the back of the heart. The right coronary artery curls around the right side and back of the heart, bringing blood to those regions.

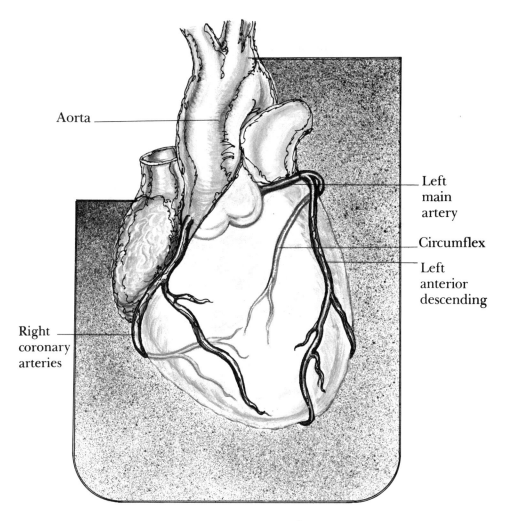

Aorta

Left
main
artery

Circumflex

Left
anterior
descending

Right
coronary
arteries

The coronary arteries

The Beat Goes On

The heart beats about 100,000 times a day, with only a
fraction of a second rest between beats—a great deal of
work. Most adults experience about 60 to 100 contractions a minute.

What causes these contractions is the heart's electrical system, which produces the normal rhythmic beating. A small group of cells, called the *sinus node* and located in the right atrium, send electrical impulses across the heart muscle, stimulating the muscles of the atrium and then those of the ventricle. When so stimulated, the muscle walls contract, pumping the blood throughout the cardiovascular system. With it all, the heart pumps over 4,000 gallons of blood through the body each day.

Now, let us see how this knowledge of the heart can help you understand your own heart or coronary disorder. You need not read all of Chapters 6 through 10, only those that seem to apply to you.

CHAPTER 6

Clogged Pipes: Atherosclerosis and Coronary Disease

How did your heart and blood vessels get to the state that they are in today? In all likelihood, it started when you were much younger, perhaps even in childhood. A narrowing or blocking of certain arteries began developing, caused by a condition known as *atherosclerosis,* commonly referred to as "hardening of the arteries" or "arteriosclerosis."

Atherosclerosis consists of fatty substances and other particles within the bloodstream collecting on the normally smooth inside walls of the arteries. The precise cause of this condition is not always known, but it may partly be due to or become worse as the result of smoking, high blood pressure, or excessive amounts of cholesterol in your diet.

As these fatty substances accumulate, usually over a period of many years, the build-up becomes progressively

thicker, and the channel inside the artery becomes stead-
ily narrowed (see the illustration). In addition, the blood
may stick to these fatty substances and clot, causing further clogging of the channel. (This blood clot is called a
thrombus.)

The result of this narrowing is, of course, an interference in the flow of blood, which means certain tissues
in your body aren't getting enough oxygen and other
nutrients.

Progressive obstruction of artery from atherosclerosis

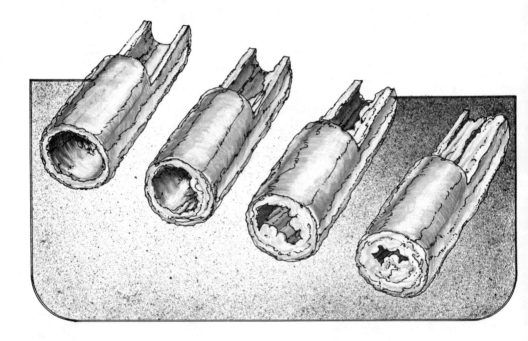

Effects of Atherosclerosis on the Heart

When an accumulation of these fatty substances, waste materials, or blood clots stops or severely restricts the flow of blood through the coronary arteries (the arteries of the heart itself), it may have two principal effects:

- *Angina pectoris:* There may be a temporary inadequacy in the supply of blood needed to meet the requirements of the heart tissue. This situation can cause feelings of pain or discomfort in the chest, called angina pectoris or simply "angina." The symptoms are temporary, and no permament changes nor damage to the heart muscle occurs.

- *Myocardial infarction:* Otherwise known as a "heart attack," "coronary," or "coronary thrombosis," this occurs when the blood supply becomes so restricted that it actually causes injury to the heart muscle.

It is possible to have coronary artery disease and *not* experience angina or a heart attack, either because the narrowing of the arteries is not severe enough to interfere with the nutrition of the heart or because there are enough other arteries in the heart so that, when one is blocked, the blood is routed to the same area through another, nearby artery. In addition, if one coronary artery fails, a nearby one may establish new branches to service the deprived area of the heart. This development of cross-connecting branches is termed *collateral circulation*—see the illustration on the next page.

Angina pectoris, myocardial infarction, and other consequences of coronary disease, such as rate and rhythm disturbances and congestive failure, are described in greater detail in the next four chapters.

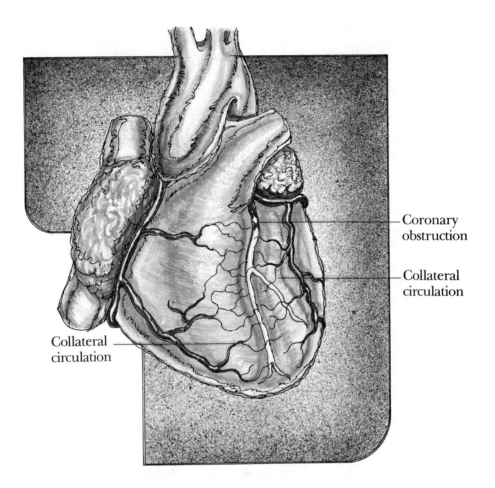

Coronary
obstruction

Collateral
circulation

Collateral
circulation

Other Problems Caused by Atherosclerosis

Atherosclerosis may also cause:

- *Stroke*—blockage in an artery supplying the brain, resulting in temporary or permanent damage and man-
ifesting itself as some form of sudden paralysis or defect in speech or vision.

- *Blockage of the kidney artery*—causing kidney failure or high blood pressure.

- *Blockage in arteries to the legs*—causing pain in the calf, thigh or buttock, especially when walking.

Serious as atherosclerosis can be, it is a condition familiar to your physician. Between the two of you and the therapy we plan to lay out in this book, there is a reasonable chance it can be stabilized.

Physical activity   Emotional tension   Cold weather   Heavy meals

Conditions triggering episodes of angina

CHAPTER 7

Chest Distress:
Angina Pectoris

W HEN you run for a bus or get into an argument, you're probably aware (at least afterwards) of your heart working especially hard: the heart demands more energy-producing fuel (oxygen and other nutrients) as it beats more vigorously and rapidly. Conversely, when you are sleeping or relaxed, the heart doesn't need to work particularly hard and it requires much less in the way of fuel.

When no coronary disease is present, the coronary arteries are able to supply an amount of blood to the heart muscle appropriate to its need. However, when coronary disease is present, the blood flow to the heart muscle is potentially restricted, and the more severe the coronary narrowing, the more limited the fuel supply to the heart. Although adequate amounts of blood may reach the heart muscle when you're relatively inactive, under circumstances of activity or anxiety a condition termed *coronary insufficiency* may develop. As the heart pumps more vigorously, not enough blood is able to reach the heart muscle because of the narrowed arteries. This may produce the chest pain, *angina pectoris.*

Symptoms

The symptoms of angina vary considerably, and may be felt as a mild, vague feeling by some people and as a severe pain by others. Among the most commonly reported symptoms are a dull, pressing, weightlike, burning or constricting sensation in the mid-chest or solar plexus. The pain may remain in the center of the chest or it may spread to the neck, lower jaw, shoulders, or down into either arm (more commonly the left arm) toward the elbow. It's a little different in everyone.

These symptoms, which are frequently brought on by heavy exertion, emotional stress, or activity following a heavy meal or during cold weather, generally last several minutes.

Don't Be Fooled

Not every chest pain or ache is due to coronary disease or angina pectoris. Other conditions which are *not serious* often occur that may produce similar symptoms, which can be frightening and may make you think you are having angina or a heart attack. For example:

- Muscular spasms in the chest wall, often sharp or stabbing pains in a small area on one side of the chest.

- Diseases of the stomach or other parts of the gastrointestinal tract, including acid indigestion, ulcers, gallbladder disease.

- Abnormalities of the spine.

- Pericarditis and pleurisy—inflammation of the sac surrounding the heart or lungs.

- Simple worry or anxiety.

When in doubt, check with your physician for proper diagnosis. No need to worry needlessly.

Changes in the Frequency and Severity of Angina

Many patients have angina lasting for years, yet they are only minimally limited and never suffer a heart attack. Indeed, the angina may even disappear. However, sometimes it may become more severe, and, if precipitously worse, may precede a heart attack. And sometimes it may occur during hospitalization for a heart attack or appear after a patient is released from the hospital following an attack.

Angina can be a possible *warning* of a more urgent condition, if the following occur:

- It becomes more severe over a period of time or develops with increasing frequency.

- It occurs as the result of progressively less activity or exertion.

- It persists after you have been discharged from the hospital following a heart attack.

- It begins to develop at night, waking you from a sound sleep.

- It persists for more than 10 to 15 minutes.

- The pain is severe enough to cause unusual perspiration.

- It is not readily relieved by rest or by taking more than three nitroglycerin tablets or the usually prescribed amount of nitroglycerin.

None of these signs is an absolute indicator of an impending problem, but you should check with your physician to be sure. If the discomfort is reasonably severe or unusual, have someone drive you to a nearby hospital emergency room. Your doctor or the staff on duty there can evaluate the situation and decide if there is cause for concern.

Treatment

Among the drugs commonly used to treat angina pectoris are nitroglycerin, some long-acting nitroglycerin-like drugs termed nitrates, and propranolol. Their objective is to reduce the demand by the heart for oxygen and other nutrients.

Nitroglycerin and other long-acting nitrates help drop the blood pressure and decrease the amount of blood the heart has to pump, thereby reducing the amount of oxygen required to nourish the heart muscle, so the angina pain often disappears. Nitroglycerin is taken under the tongue during an angina attack to speed the disappearance of the pain. Don't be worried about taking nitroglycerin; it's not dangerous or habit forming and won't lose its strength with repeated use. The longer-acting nitrates are taken at regular intervals, say, every 3, 6 or 12 hours, to *prevent* the recurrence of the pain.

Propranolol slows the heart rate and diminishes the vigor of the heart muscle contraction, thereby decreasing its workload and consequent demand for a large blood and oxygen supply, so that the angina is decreased or disappears.

Another treatment, designed to lessen the likelihood of further narrowing of the coronary arteries, is to eliminate principal risk factors by controlling high blood pressure, stopping smoking, beginning an exercise program, and providing a low-cholesterol diet or a weight-reducing diet. These are described later. Sometimes coronary bypass surgery is required for stubborn angina cases; this is discussed in Chapter 24.

The Future

Angina pectoris may be uncomfortable or frankly disabling, but it is eminently subject to successful therapy.

The symptoms can be effectively treated in most cases, the dangers may be minimized, and steps can be taken to prevent the problem from progressing.

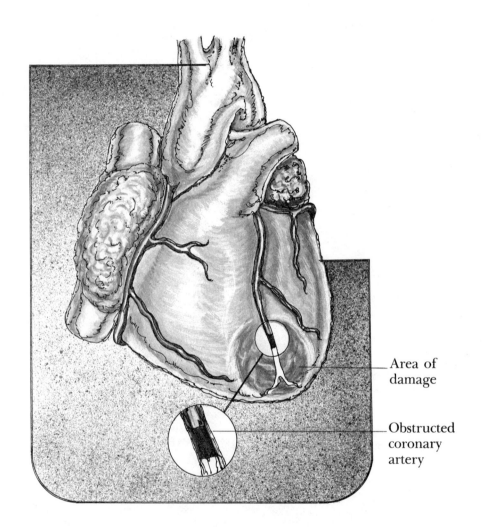

Area of
damage

Obstructed
coronary
artery

CHAPTER **8**

Heart Attack: The M.I.

T HE classic picture most people have of someone with a heart attack is of that person in an agony of pain ("the worst pain I've ever felt," some have described it), and indeed this may be the case. Yet, surprisingly, often there may be very little pain or discomfort during a heart attack.

What is a heart attack exactly? It happens when a coronary artery has become severely narrowed by atherosclerosis and also, possibly, when a small clot of blood settles on top of the fatty substance on the walls of the artery. When the attack occurs, an area of the heart muscle becomes damaged because of a lack of blood supply. This heart attack is called a "myocardial infarction," "M.I.," "coronary," or "coronary thrombosis."

Symptoms

As we indicated in Chapter 1, a heart attack may become apparent to you in a variety of ways:

- It may cause pain in the chest or just below the rib cage in the solar plexus, occasionally spreading to one or both shoulders or upper arms, and may last for minutes or even hours. As mentioned, the discomfort may be rather mild, perhaps totally unnoticed, or it may be severe and may be accompanied by sweating, nausea, vomiting, weakness, or fainting.
- It may cause disturbances of the *rhythm of the heart* (see Chapter 9), either inconsequential or serious enough to require therapy—so serious they may occasionally lead to the heart's stopping. If this didn't happen within the first few hours, chances are it won't.
- It may cause interference with the pumping action of the heart, resulting in symptoms of *congestive heart failure* (see Chapter 10) or in a fall in blood pressure.

If you suspect you're having a heart attack, don't delay. Immediately call your doctor or go to a nearby emergency room. No harm is done if some of these turn out to be false alarms.

Treatment

During the first few days (and especially the first few hours) following a myocardial infarction, the damaged heart is particularly sensitive, and any undue activity may bring about more chest pain, change in blood pressure, or heart-rhythm irregularity. Thus, complete bed rest is usually necessary for two or three days. During this time, and in the weeks to follow, the heart's own reparative processes begin to work, eventually forming a strong scar in the damaged tissue and strengthening nearby heart muscle.

Doctors don't prescribe bed rest or limited activity without reason. Just as putting a broken arm in a cast allows the bone to rest and repair itself, so reducing the heart's activity gives the injured tissue greater opportunity for recovery. Moreover, the heart is especially weak the first few days after the heart attack, and the reparative process allows it to become stronger as the weeks pass.

A number of medications are commonly used to treat myocardial infarctions, some administered in pill form, some by injections, and some by intravenous infusions. Medications are utilized to strengthen the heartbeat, modify the blood pressure, control rhythm disturbances, and to make you more pain free and allow you to sleep.

The Future

Heart attacks vary greatly in the amount of damage done. Some myocardial infarctions are quite small and produce few long-term consequences—after recovery you can essentially return to a normal way of living. Other attacks are somewhat larger, and you may be obliged to modify your working and living habits to some degree in the months to come. In some cases the heart attack is so severe—with persisting congestive heart failure, angina, or rhythm disturbances (see the individual chapters on these subjects)—that substantial modifications must be made in activities and occupation. The point to remember, though, is that *most people* who have had a heart attack return to an active and productive way of life.

The heart generally completes its reparative processes in two or three months. As we will show, this is not just time on your hands. There are a number of important programs to undertake to help you in your comeback.

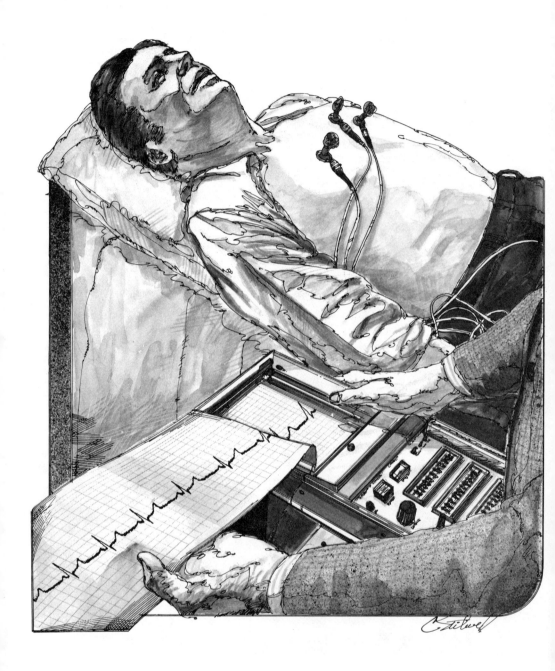

CHAPTER 9

Out of Sync: Rate and Rhythm Disturbances

If you've ever had too many cups of coffee or cigarettes or drinks, you may have noticed your heart seemed to "skip a beat"—that is, experience premature or early heart beats (called *extrasystoles*). Sometimes such skipped beats seem to happen for no particular reason at all, but in any case they are not an unusual occurrence, even in people with normal hearts, and are no cause for alarm.

The heart has its own electrical system, which produces an evenly timed, regular, clocklike beat. When relaxed, most adults have a heart rate between 60 and 80 beats per minute—slower if they are in good physical shape. Of course the heart beats faster (100–150 or more) during strenuous activity or emotional stress and slower during sleep or meditation.

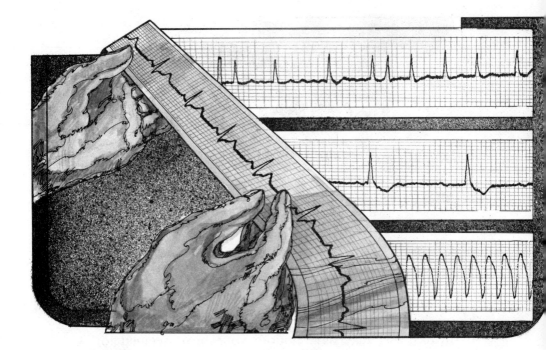

Rhythm Disturbances Due to Heart Attack

A heart-attack patient, however, may experience one of several rate and rhythm disturbances, which, if untreated, could become dangerous:

- Irregular heart rhythms: including increasingly frequent premature beats (also termed ectopic beats or extrasystoles) and atrial fibrillation (a totally irregular beat).

- Slower than normal heart rate (bradycardia).

- Faster than normal heart rate (tachycardia).

Let us consider these.

Irregular Beating of the Heart (Extrasystoles and Fibrillation)

SYMPTOMS. Sometimes a heart attack can cause an irregularity in the heart's rhythm. Premature, or early, heartbeats (extrasystoles) can occur infrequently—that is, less than a few times a minute—or may appear with increasing frequency—more than 10 or 20 times per minute. Premature beats may actually lead to a very fast heart rate, a tachycardia. In atrial fibrillation, the rhythm of the heart is totally irregular and at times the heart beats excessively rapidly.

TREATMENT. Rare premature beats may require no therapy, whereas more frequent ones are treated with rhythm-suppressing drugs, such as lidocaine (Xylocaine) or procainamide. These are drugs administered intravenously which suppress premature contractions and prevent the appearance of a tachycardia. In some coronary care units, lidocaine is given even if no premature beats are seen, to *prevent* the emergence of potentially serious rhythm disturbances.

When premature beats occur after the first several days of the heart attack, they may be treated by drugs in pill form, such as propranolol, quinidine, or procainamide, which can suppress or correct irregular heart rhythm. Atrial fibrillation is treated with either a digitalis preparation or propranolol to slow the heart rate or with one of the antiarrhythmic drugs (quinidine, procainamide, or propranolol) to abolish this irregularity of rhythm.

Rapid Heartbeat (Tachycardia)

SYMPTOMS. As indicated earlier, the heart rate will normally increase during physical activity or emotion, in order to supply more blood to the body tissues. There are times, however, when, unrelated to these normal conditions, the heart may spontaneously begin to beat excessively rapidly—a condition termed tachycardia. In many cases, this situation is of little or no concern and may quickly correct itself. In other cases, it may lead to there being a shortage of blood delivered to the tissues and a fall of blood pressure.

Among the symptoms of tachycardia are palpitations, a sense that the heart is racing, skipping, or beating irregularly; the feeling of faintness, weakness, confusion, or upset stomach, owing to reduced blood supply to the tissues; shortness of breath, because of the backing up of blood in the lungs; or chest pain, if an inadequate amount of blood is reaching the heart muscle.

TREATMENT.   The same medications used to treat irregular heart rhythms are used to treat the tachycardias. In addition, in certain cases of tachycardia and atrial fibrillation, it may be necessary to apply an electrical shock to the patient's chest (often called *cardioversion*) in order to cause the heart to resume its normal pace.

Slow Heartbeat (Bradycardia)

SYMPTOMS.   When the heart slows down to rates below 45 to 50 beats per minute, it may (like tachycardia) lead to a deficiency of blood reaching the tissues. The blood pressure may fall, and one may feel dizziness, faintness, or confusion. Symptoms similar to those seen in tachycardia may also appear. One cause of a very slow heart rate is termed *heart block,* where an interruption of the electrical transmission in the heart takes place.

TREATMENT.   As is true of irregular rhythms and tachycardia, slowing of the heart may require no therapy at all. In rare instances, a drug such as atropine or isoproterenol (Isuprel) may be injected in order to speed the heart.

In addition, when a patient has a very slow heart that does not respond to drug therapy, an electrical *pacemaker* may be used to speed the electrical impulses to the heart and cause it to contract at a normal rate (see illustration).

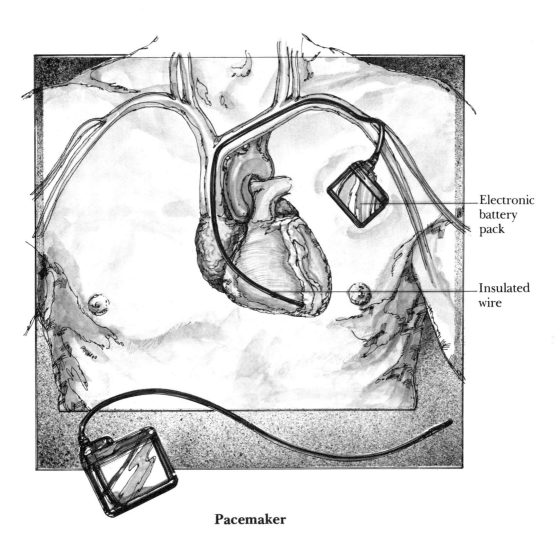

Electronic battery pack

Insulated wire

Pacemaker

This is a compact battery system, designed to deliver a series of small electrical impulses to the heart muscle, usually at the rate of 60 to 75 times a minute. The pacemaker is connected to the heart with an insulated wire which passes through a vein to lie against the inner surface of the heart. Each electrical impulse from the pacemaker causes the heart to contract or beat.

The Future

The disturbed heart rhythms, such as premature beats, atrial fibrillation, tachycardia, and bradycardia, may cause problems when they occur during or after a heart attack. Fortunately, the development of efficient cardiac monitoring equipment for the coronary care unit in the hospital to detect these abnormal rhythms has made early discovery and treatment possible and has resulted in a dramatic decrease in the number of fatalities from heart attacks among hospitalized patients.

Moreover, the physicians and nurses in the coronary care unit are trained specifically to recognize and treat rate and rhythm disturbances that may occur following a heart attack. There is always someone watching the heart monitors and ready to deal with any emergency. Today, CCU patients seldom have rhythm disturbances that cannot be readily corrected.

CHAPTER **10**

Problems Down at the Pump: Congestive Heart Failure

T HE term "heart failure" is an unfortunate one—as well as misleading and frightening—since it certainly should not imply the heart has stopped or is in danger of stopping. However, *congestive heart failure* is the name given to the condition in which, when the heart muscle is weakened and its ability to pump impaired, blood backs up into the tissues and there is an inadequate supply of blood and nutrients delivered to the rest of the body.

This heart failure may be caused by a heart attack (from the damaged heart muscle), persistent high blood pressure (owing to the long-time pressure load under which the heart has been forced to labor), or a variety of other disorders, including rheumatic fever, birth defects of the heart, and other diseases not discussed here. Whatever the cause, the effect is that the normal ability of the heart to pump blood declines, and the body begins to retain excessive quantities of salt and water.

Symptoms

Congestive heart failure may become apparent in the following ways:

- Fluids collect in the lungs and limbs.

- As these fluids accumulate, the lungs become congested, and shortness of breath results. This difficulty in breathing most commonly occurs after some physical activity, although it can also develop when you are lying down and be so severe that it may awaken you from a sound sleep, and you may find it necessary to prop yourself up in bed.

- Because fluids begin to seep through the thin walls of the capillaries and accumulate in the tissues, a swelling called *edema* develops in the ankles, legs, and sometimes even the abdomen. Edema is frequently first noticed as a tightness of shoes or clothing.

Treatment

Besides restricting your salt intake, your physician may prescribe the following medications:

- Different forms of digitalis, including digoxin and digitoxin—drugs that increase the pumping action (strength of contraction) of the heart.

- Diuretics or water pills—of which many types are available. These act to remove excessive amounts of salt and water from the body by causing increases in the amount of urination.

- Drugs that reduce the load on the heart. Some medicines that lower blood pressure and many of the nitrates (the same ones used for angina) permit the heart to contract more effectively.

The Future

Many patients feel tired or short of breath following a heart attack, not because of the heart's failure to pump effectively, but because they are out of condition—they have lost their normal body tone as the result of days and weeks of inactivity. There may also be anxiety arising from the stresses of the attack, and this, too, will cause fatigue.

If you have this kind of trouble, check it out with a physician to see whether or not it is heart failure. Even if it is, the danger is often not nearly as severe as it sounds, and appropriate therapy is generally available.

CHAPTER **11**

Taking Risks: Your Habits Matter

H EART disease is as American as apple pie. Or maybe we should say as American as bacon and eggs.

We have one of the highest rates of heart disease in the world (Finland is higher), and this is not without reason. To a large degree it is because of the way we live. While we often act as though our habits don't matter, it is clear that they do. And some of these habits drastically increase the risk of heart disease.

Risk factors are conditions that contribute to the development of cardiovascular disease. There are two kinds of risks—controllable and noncontrollable.

Noncontrollable Risks

Among the risks you can't control are your age, your sex, and your heredity. Coronary disease becomes more common as people grow older, it is more common among men than women—at least until women reach the menopause—and it is more common among people whose close relatives have had cardiovascular disease. O.K., you can't do anything about that. What can you control?

Controllable Risks

Two risks that can be controlled with your physician's help are high blood pressure and diabetes. Among the risk factors that *you* can do something about are: cigarette smoking, cholesterol intake, excess weight, inactivity, and a few other things we'll go over.

By far and away, the most important risk factors, according to a major study in Framingham, Massachusetts, are *cigarette smoking, high blood pressure,* and *cholesterol.* These are such powerful risks they are often termed the "Big Three." And all of these risks can add up. Leaving more than one risk factor uncontrolled is a considerably bigger gamble than leaving just a single one.

And if you have a family history of cardiovascular disease, this may be because you or your relatives tend to have high cholesterol or high blood pressure, so that a so-called noncontrollable risk, heredity, may in fact be within your control.

Some people think that coffee is a risk, but several studies have uniformly failed to show that coffee drinking has harmful effects on the cardiovascular system.

Diabetes: Another Risk

Are you possibly a diabetic? If you have been hospitalized with a heart condition, your doctor has probably determined whether you are or aren't. If you don't know, try the questionnaire opposite. It takes only a minute.

Diabetes is a remarkably silent disease, and this is important: *One of two people with diabetes doesn't even realize he or she has it.*

Thus, maybe you're a diabetic and don't know it. Check with your physician to be sure.

Are You a Possible Diabetic?

Take 30 seconds to answer the questions on this check-list:

	YES	NO
1. Any diabetics in your family?	☐	☐
2. Are you over 40?	☐	☐
3. Are you overweight?	☐	☐
4. Any sudden weight loss?	☐	☐
5. Are you constantly thirsty?	☐	☐
6. Do you overeat?	☐	☐
7. Do you urinate too frequently?	☐	☐
8. Do you tire easily?	☐	☐
9. Do your wounds heal slowly?	☐	☐
10. Any tingling, numbness, or pains in your fingers or toes?	☐	☐
11. Any changes in vision?	☐	☐
12. Does your skin itch frequently?	☐	☐
13. Women: have you had a baby weighing over nine pounds at birth?	☐	☐

Interpretation: Every "yes" answer to the above quiz raises the possibility of your being a diabetic.

What is diabetes? It's a disorder in which the body does not make proper use of sugar, so that there is too much sugar in the bloodstream and the body therefore runs less efficiently.

People who have diabetes have a much greater chance of developing coronary disease—and of developing it when they are young—as well as having stroke, kidney disorders, and vessel diseases in the legs.

If you think diabetes is uncommon, that's not true. It strikes 5 percent of the population—6 million Americans a year. It most often develops in persons over 40; however, since it runs in families, even youngsters can get it.

Diabetes can be checked with proper exercise, by eating the right amounts of foods at the right time, and, if necessary, with insulin administration, although most adults with diabetes don't need insulin.

The Pill

Another risk factor that you can control is birth-control pills, which have been linked to the early development of heart attack, stroke, and high blood pressure. In addition, these pills may cause inflammation of the veins of the legs, a disease called *thrombophlebitis.* This condition in turn can be the cause of another disease called *pulmonary embolism,* which may result when a blood clot formed in a vein breaks off and travels in the bloodstream to a lung, where it blocks an artery.

Women on birth-control pills have a severalfold greater likelihood of having heart attacks than do women not on the pill. Furthermore, oral contraceptives may *add* to the risk produced by other factors such as cigarette smoking, high blood pressure, or high cholesterol levels. Thus, if one or more of these is present in your life and you take birth-control pills besides, your chances of suffering a coronary or stroke go up even higher.

So what do we recommend about birth-control pills? First of all, no one, not even a healthy person, should take them without checking with her doctor. While it's probably O.K. for young women to take them for awhile, if you are over 40 or have some of the other risk factors in your life or, of course, if you have already suffered a heart attack or stroke, oral contraceptives are best avoided.

Evaluating Your Chances

The table on the following page is not magical, is not a scientifically proven means of accurately estimating one's chances for developing cardiovascular disease. However, at least it gives you some ball-park idea of where you stand. We urge you to grab a pencil and take a moment to determine what your risk profile is. For each risk factor, select the statement that most closely fits you, and then add the score located at the bottom of each column. Your total score then provides an estimate of your risk of developing cardiovascular problems.

After you've completed your profile, read those of Chapters 12 through 18 that seem to apply to you, to see how you can manage these risk factors.

Cardiovascular Disease (CD) Risk Calculator

NONCONTROLLABLE RISK FACTORS

Heredity	No family history	1–2 close relatives (parent or sibling develop CD over age 60)	1–2 close relatives (parent or sibling develop CD under age 60)
Sex	Female (premenopausal)	—	Male or postmeno-pausal female
Age	10–20	21–40	41–50

CONTROLLABLE RISK FACTORS

Controllable with physician's help

Blood pressure (systolic)	Under 120	120–139	140–159
Diabetes	No	—	—

Controllable with self-help

Cigarettes	No	Inhaled pipe or cigars	Under ½ pack per day
Blood cholesterol	Under 170	170–199	200–219
Body weight	Under standard	Standard	5–15 lb. over
Exercise	Vigorous (job or recreational)	Active (job or recreation)	—
SCORE	0	1	2

Several relatives (including aunts or uncles; some develop CD under age 55)	—	—	—
—	—	—	—
Over 50	—	—	—
160–179	180–199	200–229	Over 230
Yes	—	—	—
½–1 pack per day	—	1–2 packs per day	Over 2 packs per day
220–239	240–269	270–299	Over 300
16–25 lb. over	26–50 lb. over	More than 50 lb. over	—
Sedentary	—	—	—
3	4	5	6

YOUR SCORE	YOUR RISK PROFILE
Under 10	Very low
10–14	Low
15–20	Moderately increased
21–24	High
Over 25	Very high

CHAPTER 12

Stress

T HERE is an interesting phenomenon as regards this "risk
factor." Public-opinion surveys show that Americans be-
lieve *stress* is the most important cause of coronary heart
disease—more important, in fact, than high blood pressure, smoking, or diet. The popularity of this idea is no
doubt one of the reasons why so many people don't pay
attention to the other risk factors. (They also get little in
the way of good advice from the advertising by the tobacco, dairy, and egg industries.)

But does stress really contribute to heart disease? A
few physicians assert that the trials and tribulations of
modern life—job pressures, family squabbles, money
problems, illness of a relative, for example—add up to a
big risk factor. Others say the problem is internal; it is
how strongly you personally react to outside annoyances
and pressures that determines your liability.

Type A Behavior?

Indeed, some investigators have gone so far as to classify
two types of behavior, Type A and Type B. Type A per-

sonalities are competitive, hard-driving individuals, both at work and at play. They are constantly concerned about time and are easily irritated, so that when they are caught behind a slow driver or made to wait in a restaurant, for example, they begin to boil inside. The Type B person, by contrast, is calmer and more relaxed, able to take life as it comes. Of course, the latter type, it is thought by these investigators, is less apt to get a heart attack.

What do we think of all this? We are not sure. The reports linking stress or behavior type to risk are too scanty. They have not been corroborated by other independent investigators working in the same field. One problem, for example, has been the difficulty in accurately measuring each person's "stress score." And certainly classifying people as being either Type A or Type B seems to be an oversimplification: everybody has traits on both sides of the fence. We are not Type A *or* Type B; we are a little of each.

Moreover, studies of life-styles in various cultures do not confirm the stress hypothesis. The Japanese live and work amongst crowded, competitive, time-urgent conditions, yet their rate of coronary disease is extremely low. By contrast, some of the highest rates in the world have been found among Finnish loggers and farmers, who lead quiet outdoor lives. Finally, a great amount of atherosclerotic disease was found among a group of American railroad workers who had apparently adapted well to a paternalistic, friendly employer and were not living in a state of struggle and time urgency. In short, there is going to have to be more research on the subject of stress before we can conclude that it is a true coronary risk.

While we are waiting for this information, what can we tell our patients? Let's take the commonsense approach: You have had a heart attack or have coronary disease. In making your comeback, you know that some things will probably have to change as far as diet, exercise, and the like. While you are revising your behavior in those areas, it makes sense to revise it in the area of stress, too. Stress, after all, is what makes a lot of people smoke too much, drink too much, and eat too much—and *those* factors may very well contribute to coronary problems. There will always be problems and pressures, of course, but at least you can begin to make a pact with yourself that you won't "overreact" next time you get behind a slow truck on a mountain road or can't catch your waiter's eye. Life is better when it is calmer.

Your Stress Profile

To get an idea how much stress you have in your life, try taking the following quizzes.

Stress Behavior Quiz

Circle the number on the scale below that best characterizes your behavior for each trait.

Trait	Scale	
1. Casual about appointments	1 2 3 4 5 6 7 8	Never late
2. Not competitive	1 2 3 4 5 6 7 8	Very competitive
3. Never feel rushed, even under pressure	1 2 3 4 5 6 7 8	Always rushed
4. Take things one at a time	1 2 3 4 5 6 7 8	Try to do many things at once, think about what you are going to do next
5. Slow doing things	1 2 3 4 5 6 7 8	Fast (eating, walking, etc.)
6. "Sit" on feelings	1 2 3 4 5 6 7 8	Express feelings
7. Many interests	1 2 3 4 5 6 7 8	Few interests outside work

Total your score: ____   Multiply it by 3: _____

Interpretation:

Less than 90	Calm
90–99	Moderately calm
100–105	Stressful
106–119	Moderately stressful
120 or more	Very stressful

Source: Adapted with permission from *Journal of Chronic Diseases* 22 (1969): 87–91, by R. W. Bortner, "A Short Rating Scale as a Potential Measure of Pattern A Behavior"; copyright 1969 Pergamon Press, Ltd.

Testing Your Life Stresses

Which of the following have you had within the last two years? Circle the number on the right.

LIFE EVENT	MEAN VALUE
1. Death of spouse	100
2. Divorce	73
3. Marital separation from mate	65
4. Detention in jail or other institution	63
5. Death of a close family member	63
6. Major personal injury or illness	53
7. Marriage	50
8. Being fired at work	47
9. Marital reconciliation with mate	45
10. Retirement from work	45
11. Major change in the health or behavior of a family member	44
12. Pregnancy	40
13. Sexual difficulties	39
14. Gaining a new family member (e.g., through birth, adoption, oldster moving in, etc.)	39
15. Major business readjustment (e.g., merger, reorganization, bankruptcy, etc.)	39
16. Major change in financial state (e.g., a lot worse off or a lot better off than usual)	38
17. Death of a close friend	37
18. Changing to a different line of work	36
19. Major change in the number of arguments with spouse (e.g., either a lot more or a lot less than usual regarding child-rearing, personal habits, etc.)	35
20. Taking on a mortgage greater than $10,000 (e.g., purchasing a home, business, etc.)	31
21. Foreclosure on a mortgage or loan	30
22. Major changes in responsibilities at work (e.g., promotion, demotion, lateral transfer)	29
23. Son or daughter leaving home (e.g., marriage, attending college, etc.)	29
24. In-law troubles	29

25. Outstanding personal achievement   28
26. Wife beginning or ceasing work outside the home   26
27. Beginning or ceasing formal schooling   26
28. Major change in living conditions (e.g., building a new
    home, remodeling, deterioration of home or neighborhood)   25
29. Revision of personal habits (dress, manners, associations, etc.)   24
30. Troubles with the boss   23
31. Major change in working hours or conditions   20
32. Change in residence   20
33. Changing to a new school   20
34. Major change in usual type and/or amount of recreation   19
35. Major change in church activities (e.g., a lot more or a lot
    less than usual)   19
36. Major change in social activities (e.g., clubs, dancing, movies,
    visiting, etc.)   18
37. Taking on a mortgage or loan less than $10,000 (e.g., purchasing
    a car, TV, freezer, etc.)   17
38. Major change in sleeping habits (a lot more or a lot less sleep,
    or change in part of day when asleep)   16
39. Major change in number of family get-togethers (e.g., a lot more
    or a lot less than usual)   15
40. Major change in eating habits (a lot more or a lot less food intake,
    or very different meal hours or surroundings)   15
41. Vacation   13
42. Christmas   12
43. Minor violations of the law (e.g., traffic tickets, jaywalking,
    disturbing the peace, etc.)   11

Total score: _____

Interpretation:

0–149	Low stress
150–199	Mild stress
200–299	Moderate stress
300 or more	Major stress

Source: T. H. Holmes and R. H. Rahe, "The Social Readjustment Rating Scale," *Journal of Psychosomatic Research* II (1967): 213–18.

CHAPTER 13

High Blood Pressure

MANY people think they can tell high blood pressure is present by headaches or other symptoms, but the only way to know if this is true is to have it measured—with a pressure cuff attached to a measuring device called a sphygmomanometer (*sfig-mo-mah-NOM-e-ter*), which describes the blood pressure in terms of two numbers: *systolic* and *diastolic*.

Systolic pressure (the first number) is a measure of the tension on the artery walls caused by the beating heart pumping blood into the arteries.

Diastolic pressure is a measure of the tension remaining between heartbeats.

Find out from your doctor or nurse what your blood pressure is and write it down here:

_____/_____.

The average blood pressure reading for adults is about 120 systolic and 80 diastolic. This is called "120 over 80" and is generally written "120/80." Blood pressure varies somewhat, depending on activity. Usually, it is lower when you're at rest and higher when you're active, excited, or under stress. Normal blood pressure under relaxed conditions should be below 150/90, but 160/95 is probably acceptable in people in their 70s and over.

However, when blood pressure goes up and *stays there,* the condition is called *hypertension* or "high blood pressure." Hypertension should not be confused with "nervousness," a hyperactive personality, or with a blushing complexion. It simply means high pressure within the artery.

Where do you stand? The chart below shows the chances of having a heart attack depending on one's *systolic* blood pressure.

The Risk of Having a Heart Attack If You Have High Blood Pressure

A person whose blood pressure at systole (when the heart contracts) is over 150 has more than two times the risk of heart attack of a person with systolic blood pressure under 120.

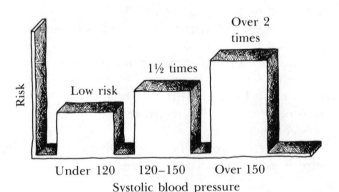

Source: Extrapolated from American Heart Association data, based on the Framingham, Mass., Heart Study.

In most cases, the cause of hypertension is unknown, though occasionally abnormalities of the kidneys, the blood vessels feeding them, or certain substances in the bloodstream may be at fault. High blood pressure also runs in families, so if one of your parents had it, there is a chance you can develop it, too.

High blood pressure occurs when the artery walls squeeze down excessively on the blood that flows by, thereby raising the pressure. The danger of this is that, over the years, this excessive pressure can wear out the arteries and, if not treated, can lead to strokes, coronary artery disease, congestive heart failure, visual difficulties, and diseases of the kidneys. It can also aggravate angina pectoris by increasing the severity and frequency of the pain.

The good news is that hypertension is dangerous only when it is ignored or inadequately treated, and in most cases it is amenable to therapy. Sometimes it even disappears after a heart attack.

Treatment

Dieting to take off some of that excess weight, often with the aid of an exercise program, represents one means of correcting hypertension. Medication and restriction of salt intake are the two other principal approaches.

It may be possible for the physician to lower your blood pressure by prescribing only a single medication (usually in pill form), but on occasion the dose of that pill has to be raised to two or more tablets daily, and combinations of two, three, or even four different drugs are sometimes needed to bring the pressure down. The medications used to treat hypertension are described in detail in Appendix A.

The medications that are given to help bring the blood pressure down *must be taken regularly,* as frequently as prescribed by your physician, since failure to do so generally results in the blood pressure returning to its previously high levels. This is very important. The biggest difficulty with treating high blood pressure is that patients don't take their medications, don't understand them, miss doses, or get sick of (or from) them and then discontinue them. Not following the prescription *exactly* remains the major problem in the treatment of high blood pressure.

Another problem is that many of the drugs used to treat high blood pressure have *side effects,* which vary greatly in their severity and frequency from one person to another. What will happen is that your doctor will start you on a medication and, if it produces bothersome symptoms, will switch you to another drug. Thus, treatment of high blood pressure involves some trial and error.

A Salt Talk

You can also do a great deal for yourself in the treatment of hypertension, and that is to cut down on the amount of salt (sodium) you eat. Although salt is frequently mentioned in diets prepared for heart patients, it is *not* a particularly important factor in the control of coronary disease, and too many people get put on a low-salt diet who don't need it. However, high blood pressure and congestive heart failure are the two conditions where it is desirable, often mandatory, to restrict the use of salt in the diet. The reason is that salt holds onto water, overfilling the arteries and veins with water, and thus further raising the blood pressure. It can also produce swelling of the ankles or abdomen and congestion within the lungs in patients with congestive heart failure.

Although we said some people get put on low-salt diets who shouldn't be, the fact remains that Americans eat an incredible amount of salt, far more than is good for them. *We should all cut back to some degree on our salt consumption.* Foods particularly high in salt are:

- *Meats*—certain meats such as ham, bacon, sausage, lunch meats, hot dogs, corned beef, anchovies, smoked fish.
- *Cured vegetables*—certain vegetables such as french fries, potato chips, salted nuts, popcorn, pickles, relishes, olives, sauerkraut.
- *Soups*—bouillon and canned soups.
- *Condiments*—mustard, catsup, relishes, Worcestershire sauce, horseradish.
- *Other*—commercial salad dressings, party spreads and dips, pretzels, crackers, baking powder, certain cheeses, monosodium glutamate—even softened water.

Certain drugs also contain sodium, such as the alkalizers you take for stomach upset (bicarbonate of soda and Alka Seltzer).

And if you chew tobacco, you should know it is high in sodium.

The best approach to limiting your salt is:

- Don't automatically salt your food at the table.
- When cooking, flavor with spices other than salt.
- Minimize those foods highest in salt content.
- If your physician O.K.'s it, you may use a salt substitute.

Left unchecked over a period of years, hypertension can be dangerous and lead to a variety of cardiovascular and kidney diseases, but when the blood pressure is successfully lowered the danger is virtually eliminated.

CHAPTER **14**

Smoking: Playing with Fire

Lᴇᴛ's say you're a young or middle-aged woman (under 50) and healthy, with no blood-pressure problems or other disorders. Your main vice is that you smoke—say, around two packs of cigarettes a day. If so, you are *several times* more apt to have a heart attack than a nonsmoker, and there's a fifty-fifty chance it could be fatal.

Now note that we're assuming you're relatively *young, healthy,* and a *woman.* (The rate of heart attacks in the United States is four to five times higher for men than it is for women.) Although the risks go down if you smoke less, the fact remains that *smoking all by itself* can contribute to a coronary.

And, of course, we haven't even mentioned lung, throat, or tongue cancer; emphysema; stroke; and other disorders caused by cigarettes. The fact is, if you smoke two or more packs a day, you are essentially trading a minute of life for a minute of smoking. Life insurance companies know this, or they wouldn't offer reductions in premiums for nonsmokers. As the U.S. Secretary of

Health, Education, and Welfare has said, smoking is "slow-motion suicide" (see the chart below).

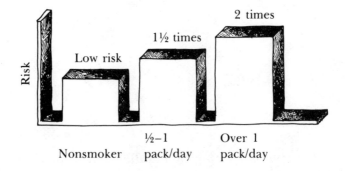

**The Risk of Having a Heart Attack
If You Smoke Cigarettes**

A person who smokes more than a pack of cigarettes a day has nearly twice the risk of heart attack of a nonsmoker.

Source: Extrapolated from American Heart Association data, based on the Framingham, Mass., Heart Study.

The way cigarettes bring on heart damage is still something of a mystery, but three possible explanations are:

- The nicotine repeatedly overstimulates the heart.
- The carbon monoxide absorbed into your blood takes the place of oxygen and hampers nourishment of the heart muscle and other tissues. People with angina pectoris develop the chest pain quicker if they smoke. Even being in the same room with people who are smoking may aggravate these chest pains.
- The smoke damages the lining of the coronary arteries, allowing artery-clogging cholesterol and other debris to build up and narrow the passageways.

Jekyll and Hyde

The good news, however, is that 5 years after you quit smoking you are statistically no more at risk than someone like you with a similar problem but who has never smoked.

Our intent is not to lecture you but to help you quit. There is no doubt that it can be difficult, though some people seem to be able to quit "cold turkey" and just suddenly give up smoking for good. The first thing that is required is *motivation*. You've got to want to do it. And the motivation must be *positive:* think how good you're going to feel, how nice the air will smell, how far and fast you will be able to run or swim. Accentuate the positive.

If you are motivated, then you have to make the decision to quit. You have to *choose*—and if you continue smoking, you should realize you are in effect choosing that smoking is more worthwhile than quitting. Have a Dr. Jekyll/Mr. Hyde debate with yourself, stating all the reasons for quitting versus not quitting.

Quitting Tips

If you have decided to quit, here are some hints:

• Be aware you will be uncomfortable for a week. However, it's O.K. to be uncomfortable. You won't suffer unbearable pain, you're not going to die from it, and the discomfort won't last. The physiological addiction, the nicotine in the body, probably lasts only 72 hours or so. Thereafter, you'll have a psychological desire to smoke; that is, a desire stemming from memories of pleasure in enjoying the cigarettes.

• As you quit smoking, your "nervous appetite" may increase, but remember this is really your desire for cigarettes in disguise. Face up to the fact. In all likelihood, if you're able to stop smoking, you're able to watch your diet, too.

- Understand that stopping smoking is a *learned skill,* just as is learning to play the violin, tennis, and so on. Thus, you can *learn* to live without cigarettes and *learn* not to crave them.

- For a few days keep a diary so you can become *aware* of when and where you smoke, and for what reasons. You will probably find there are patterns in your smoking, so you can start to do something about modifying them. If you are aware that what you really want is a cigarette, you won't necessarily end up eating that extra piece of pie (thinking erroneously that you wanted the dessert).

- Get *moral support* by making an agreement with a friend to quit at the same time. (But, beware: if your friend goes back to smoking, this could be used as an excuse by you to do the same.)

- Don't set yourself up for failure. People ask themselves, "What will happen if I become too nervous?" "What if the family gets mad at me if I fail?" "What if I start eating too much?" Many people are afraid they won't be able to work or get through the day or that they will want a cigarette so badly they will be unable to resist. Anticipating these fears makes it easier to deal with them. And don't be discouraged if you have tried but failed in stopping smoking in the past. Everyone learns something from their past attempts that gives them ammunition the next time.

Groups to Help You Quit

Many people can stop smoking on willpower alone, but if you have trouble, don't fight it. Various stop-smoking clinics and other organizations are listed under "Smokers Information and Treatment Centers" in the Yellow Pages of the phone book. Or you may want to contact your local heart association or lung society for recommendations. To an extent, each method or clinic has been successful in

getting some people to quit, but none has been demon-
strated to work for all smokers.

Among the more prominent methods are the following:

- *Some clinics stress a commonsense, positive approach*—in
  which the importance of motivation and the good that
  will come out of quitting is emphasized, and in which
  you are shown how life can go on as before—but without cigarettes.
- *Behavior modification*—in which another, more desirable
  activity (chewing gum, drawing, or whatever) is *substi-
  tuted* for the smoking. This method teaches you to avoid
  situations where you know you will want to smoke (for
  example, with coffee or while driving or sitting at the
  table after dinner) and to avoid carrying cigarettes or to
  carry them in an inconvenient place.
- *Hypnosis*—apparently successful with only a few smokers (those capable of being hypnotized) and then only
  with frequent reinforcement.
- *Aversion therapy*—in which an undesirable stimulus such
  as an electric shock is delivered to discourage you from
  smoking. A variation is to have you smoke in a small,
  poorly ventilated space to the point where it becomes
  unpleasant. This method is the least effective and not
  generally recommended.
- *Scare or fear therapy*—in which the risks are vividly dem-
  onstrated with pictures or real-life examples of patients
  with serious diseases that result from long-term smoking. This approach is seldom valuable when used alone,
  although certainly everyone should be well informed as
  to the potential hazards of smoking cigarettes.

Still, we understand that quitting cigarettes is not
easy, and you should feel free to explore any method that
seems workable to you.

One last point: while we would rather you quit smoking, if you decide it is entirely out of the question, at least try cutting down to under a half a pack a day; that's a lot safer than one or two packs per day. And try smoking cigarettes that are low in both tar and nicotine. Every little bit helps. (Caution, though: some people switch to low-nicotine cigarettes and then end up smoking twice as many as before.)

Remember that *you* hold the key to success. Either alone or with professional assistance, you must begin to deal with the stresses in your life without smoking—by understanding yourself and by believing that you truly can pull it off. Success won't last unless you keep working at it and want it to last. Good luck!

CHAPTER 15

Fat City: Cholesterol, Saturated Fats, Triglycerides

AMERICANS eat more meat per capita than people do in any European country, and only in countries with vast grazing lands such as New Zealand and Argentina is the consumption greater.

Now, although this habit might seem to date back to the American legend of cowboys and cattle drives, it is an interesting fact that meat consumption today is up *40 percent* over what it was in 1910—when the Wild West began to disappear. During that time there has also been a dramatic rise in the amount of fat consumed—up to 25 percent.

By "fat" we do not mean that stuff that, unfortunately, seems to accumulate around the waist and hips of so many of us. Here we mean *blood fats*.

There are two kinds of blood fats that are associated with cardiovascular disease and heart attack: *cholesterol* (the one that's grabbed all the headlines) and *triglycerides*. Cholesterol in particular, according to the preponderance of present medical opinion, is thought to contribute to the development of atherosclerosis, so we'll describe it first.

Cholesterol

Cholesterol is a fatlike substance found in the blood and tissues and is essential to the body function. A certain amount of it is necessary to maintain the body in proper working order, but in excess it deposits in artery linings and narrows the vessels.

How do you know if you have an excessive amount of cholesterol in your blood? A simple blood test can tell your physician. Find out what yours is from your doctor or nurse and then write it here:

_____.

Now compare your cholesterol level with the chart below to ascertain your risk.

The Risk of Having a Heart Attack If You Have a High Cholesterol Level

A person with a blood cholesterol measurement of 250 or above has about two and a half times the risk of heart attack as one with cholesterol below 194. The higher the blood cholesterol, the greater the risk of heart attack and cardiovascular disease.

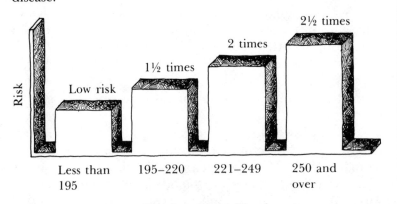

Source: Extrapolated from American Heart Association data, based on the Framingham, Mass. Heart Study.

Note from the chart below that if you have high cholesterol *and* high blood pressure *and* smoke cigarettes—what we called the Big Three risk factors—you're really taking a chance. The risk of heart attack for someone who has all these characteristics as opposed to someone who has none of them is *five times* higher.

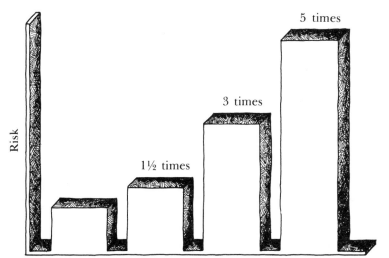

The Risk of Having a Heart Attack If You Have High Blood Pressure, Smoke Cigarettes, and Have a High Cholesterol Level—The "Big Three" Risk Factors

Risk

5 times

3 times

1½ times

No high blood pressure, high cholesterol, or cigarettes

Cigarettes

High cholesterol and cigarettes

High blood pressure, high cholesterol, and cigarettes

Source: Extrapolated from American Heart Association data, based on the Framingham, Mass. Heart Study.

Throughout the world, those peoples that consume foods containing large amounts of cholesterol and saturated fats tend on average to run higher levels of blood cholesterol and, therefore, to develop cardiovascular problems more commonly. And populations from countries that eat foods low in these substances have lower blood cholesterol and are relatively free of coronary disease.

How can you reduce your cholesterol level? By avoiding, as we shall show, two kinds of foods: (1) foods high in *cholesterol,* and (2) foods high in *saturated fats,* because the body converts these fats to cholesterol.

When we say "avoid" these foods, by the way, we don't mean you must never again have a steak or shrimp. As we said back in the chapter on doctor's orders versus doctor's recommendations, our dietary advice need not be followed rigidly. Any food may be eaten on occasion without harm—it's O.K. to have a thick steak when you're dining out on your anniversary, say. But we do recommend that you try and avoid *repeatedly* eating foods high in cholesterol and saturated fats, and learn which foods are best to substitute for those fatty ones.

We will discuss the foods high in cholesterol first and then the foods high in saturated fats.

Foods High in Cholesterol

- *Eggs.*
- *Organ meat.*
- *Shrimp.*

Let's look at each.

EGGS. Egg yolks are the single greatest source of cholesterol in the American diet. By and large, avoid them, including dishes containing eggs and foods such as egg noodles and egg breads.

Suggestion: Eat all the egg whites you wish (they contain no cholesterol). When cooking, substitute two egg whites where one egg yolk is called for. Egg substitutes are also available. Try the different brands until you find one you like. Egg Beaters, Second Nature, and Scramblers are a few on the market.

ORGAN MEAT.   All meats (including poultry and fish) contain some cholesterol, but organ meats such as liver, kidney, tongue, heart, brain, and sweetbreads contain huge amounts. Have them on special occasions but otherwise avoid.

SHRIMP.   It's O.K. to eat shrimp if you do so less than once a week or use it only as a garnish. However, be aware that it is the shellfish that contains the highest amount of cholesterol.

Foods High in Saturated Fats

There are four food groups high in saturated fats (besides the high-cholesterol foods above—eggs, organ meats, and shrimp—which are high in saturated fats as well):

• Some *meat*—including red meat and prepared meats, and stews, soups, and chili made from meat or stock.
• *Dairy products*—including certain cheeses, milk, cream, ice cream, and butter.
• *Cooking oils and fats.*
• *Convenience foods.*

Let's look at these four groups.

RED MEAT.   All of the red meats—beef, pork, lamb, and veal—contain saturated fat, which can be seen along the edges of the meat and as part of the marbling within the center. The saturated fats are greater in "prime" cuts than "choice," and least in "good" qualities. In general, pork (especially bacon and spareribs) contains more saturated fats and veal less, compared to the other red meats.

Other meats high in saturated fats are hamburger (ground round having the least—have your butcher trim and grind to order), smoked meats, and mutton.

Suggestion: Serve red meats only 3 or 4 times a week, using modest portions (approximately ⅓ pound or 5½ oz. for active working men, ¼ pound or 4 oz. for smaller and less active people). Serving up the meat on smaller plates is often helpful from a psychological standpoint. Select only the lean cuts, trim off as much fat as possible, and cook by broiling, barbecuing, roasting, or pan frying, so that the fat is allowed to run off.

PREPARED MEATS.   Almost all processed meats—hot dogs, salami, liverwurst, bologna, sausage—contain not only large amounts of saturated fat but also a lot of salt. Serve as infrequently as possible.

Suggestion: Use products low in saturated fats, such as boiled ham, chipped beef, pressed chicken, and pressed turkey. Use meat substitutes such as Fleishman's or Morningstar Farms sausage and bacon.

STEWS, SOUP, AND CHILI.   Avoid eating directly such products made from animal meat and/or stock.

Suggestion: Refrigerate overnight and then skim off the fat that has moved to the top.

CHEESE.   Since most cheeses are made from whole milk, they are reasonably high in saturated fat. Avoid Brie, Camembert, cheddar, Monterey, Muenster, Roquefort, and Swiss. Especially avoid eating large quantities of cheese.

Suggestion: Serve cheeses made from nonfat or partially skimmed milk: bakers' cheese, cottage cheese, farmers cheese, Mozzarella, sapsago, and low-fat parmesan. Cheese products low in saturated fats include: Borden's Lite-Line, Fisher Cheezola, Fisher Countdown, and Kraft's Calorie Spread.

WHOLE MILK. Whole milk is high in saturated fats. Low-fat milk contains about half the amount of fat. Nonfat has very little such fat.

Suggestion: Drink nonfat milk (and occasionally low-fat milk) instead of whole milk. Buttermilk is also acceptable.

DAIRY CREAMS. Since these are high in saturated fats, avoid all, including whipping cream, dessert cream, and half-and-half.

Suggestion: Substitute nondairy creamers (but not those made from coconut oil). For recipes requiring cream or sour cream, you may substitute a low-fat yogurt, low-fat milk, or buttermilk.

ICE CREAM. Save for special occasions.

Suggestion: Serve ice milk or, preferably, sherbert.

BUTTER. Avoid.

Suggestion: Substitute polyunsaturated margarines (in either small tubs or cubes) made from safflower, corn, soybean, or cottonseed oil. Check the labels, and use only those margarines in which the first ingredient listed shows a *liquid* oil. Avoid those that show "hydrogenated" or "partially hydrogenated" oils among the first listed ingredients, since they contain more saturated fats than the polyunsaturated margarines do. The next section explains this point.

COOKING FATS AND OILS. Certain vegetable oils such as palm and coconut oil are also high in saturated fats, as is chocolate.

A special word about *polyunsaturated fats,* which are found in vegetable oils: These do not convert into cholesterol. Indeed, they actually *lower* the amount of cholesterol in your bloodstream. The polyunsaturated fats best for you, in order of preference, are: safflower, sunflower, corn, soybean, and cottonseed.

Polyunsaturated fats are usually liquid at room temperature. But in manufacturing they may undergo "hardening" or "hydrogenation," which makes them more solid and therefore higher in saturated fat. Thus, avoid oils described on labels as "saturated," "hardened," "hydrogenated," or "partially hydrogenated." You will find these in certain peanut butters, shortening, whipped toppings, salad dressings, and hydrogenated margarines.

Suggestions: When cooking:

- Substitute polyunsaturated oils for saturated oils.
- Deep-fry foods only in polyunsaturated oils, and don't reuse the oils more than two or three times or they will become saturated.
- Instead of using chocolate (which is high in saturated fats) in recipes, use cocoa powder mixed with nonfat milk.

CONVENIENCE FOODS. Potato chips (except the polyunsaturated ones) and other fried foods, meats, and TV dinners; many cake mixes, cookies, donuts, sweetrolls, butter rolls, and muffins; and similar types of commercially available processed foods are high in saturated fat. Nuts, however, are O.K., except for cashews and macademia nuts (which are high in saturated fats).

Triglycerides

We've talked about Cholesterol and his sidekick, Saturated Fats. Now let's talk about that other blood fat, triglycerides.

These are substances that may be associated with cardiovascular disease, although the evidence is not as clear on this point as it is on cholesterol.

Having excess triglycerides may be associated with four things: inheritance of the trait (though triglycerides often don't become a problem unless one is overweight also), obesity (from consuming too many calories), excess alcohol consumption, and diabetes.

How do you know if you have too many triglycerides in your blood? As with cholesterol, a simple blood test will give your physician the information. If he or she finds your triglyceride level too high, you will probably be asked to: lose weight, start an exercise program, reduce your sugar intake, and cut down on the wine and spirits. In subsequent chapters we'll tell you how to handle those requirements.

Delectable Meals

Even if you are high in cholesterol levels, note that we aren't asking you to live on rye bread and grapefruit alone. And note also that you can eat *any* food occasionally. Most of your meals, however, can easily be made delicious and kept healthy at the same time. Some ideas:

- *Fish:* This has virtually no saturated fat. Eat it as often as you like. Shellfish (except for shrimp) is also good, if eaten only once daily.

- *Poultry:* Eat chicken and turkey as often as you like, being sure to trim the skin and its fatty underlayer before cooking. However, avoid duck and goose, and the chicken's giblets, liver, and gizzard, since they're high in saturated fat.

- *Other healthy foods:* Use natural breads, grains, cereals, and all the fresh fruits and vegetables you want. And if you're worried about not getting enough protein, because of having to cut down on meat and milk, you might try more whole grains, fruits, and vegetables, or soybean products such as tofu.

Expanding Your Culinary Horizons

If you're locked into the typical American meat-and-potatoes regimen, now's your chance to find out what the rest of the world offers. Here are some places to look for foods low in cholesterol and saturated fats: different spices, herbs, vinegars, flavorings that don't add cholesterol; Chinese or Japanese cooking; Central American and Latin American food; Middle Eastern cuisine; North African cuisine.

In exploring such areas, you'll be doing your family a favor, too. After all, our eating patterns are usually established when we are young. If you would like your children to avoid some of the things you've been through, perhaps you can start them down a different culinary path through your example. And, of course, the modifications in your diet become easier for you if everyone in the family is sharing them with you.

Check the appendixes at the end of the book. They offer valuable information to help you with your shopping and other food-related matters.

The Future

Will all this changing of diet prevent coronary disease or repeated heart attack? No one is sure. However, the wisest course would certainly seem to be the prudent course. "Eat, drink, and be merry" means eat and drink in such a way that you *can* be merry.

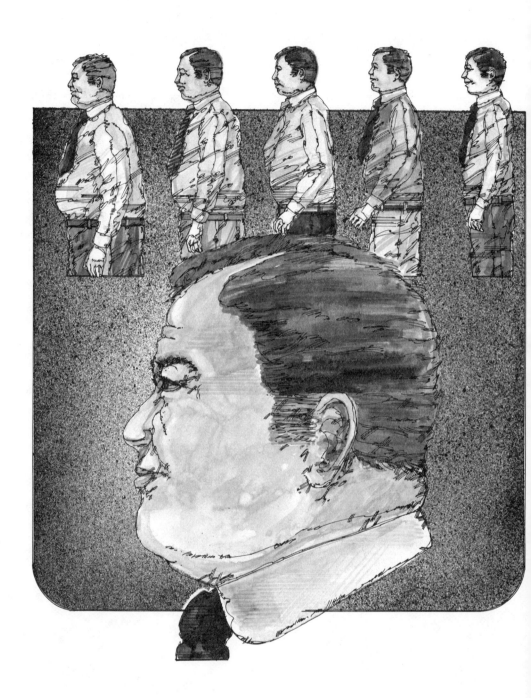

CHAPTER **16**

Take It Off

Q∪ICK, right now, pinch the skin folds over your stomach or back of your arms and see if there seems to be ½ inch or more of tissue present. If there is, it's too much. Now look at the table on the following page. It shows the new you that you could be.

Most adults in our society have a weight problem. After age 25, you end up gaining weight unless you do something about the food you eat and the amount of your daily activity. The reason is that, beginning at this age, your body starts to need less energy because your metabolism is slowing down. The result is that you require about 10 less calories every day for each year that passes, and if you don't cut back by this amount you'll end up gaining about a pound a year.

At age 26 you need 10 fewer calories than what you used to take in each day at age 25. And by age 35 your body's needs will have dropped 100 calories per day. Thus, a 45-year-old man who eats and exercises the same way he did 20 years ago will find himself weighing 20 pounds more. You don't have to eat a *lot* of extra food to

Your Ideal Weight
(Within 5- to 10-pound range)

HEIGHT (without shoes)	WEIGHT (WITHOUT CLOTHING)		
Men	Light build	Medium build	Heavy build
5 ft. 3 in.	118	129	141
5 ft. 4 in.	122	133	145
5 ft. 5 in.	126	137	149
5 ft. 6 in.	130	142	155
5 ft. 7 in.	134	147	161
5 ft. 8 in.	139	151	166
5 ft. 9 in.	143	155	170
5 ft. 10 in.	147	159	174
5 ft. 11 in.	150	163	178
6 ft.	154	167	183
6 ft. 1 in.	158	171	188
6 ft. 2 in.	162	175	192
6 ft. 3 in.	165	178	195
Women			
5 ft.	100	109	118
5 ft. 1 in.	104	112	121
5 ft. 2 in.	107	115	125
5 ft. 3 in.	110	118	128
5 ft. 4 in.	113	122	132
5 ft. 5 in.	116	125	135
5 ft. 6 in.	120	129	139
5 ft. 7 in.	123	132	142
5 ft. 8 in.	126	136	146
5 ft. 9 in.	130	140	151
5 ft. 10 in.	133	144	156
5 ft. 11 in.	137	148	161
6 ft.	141	152	166

Source: U.S. Department of Agriculture.

become fat. People who stay thin probably eat only about 3 percent less food than overweight people do.

Eating Can Be Hazardous to Your Health

Insurance company figures indicate that once you are 10 pounds over your ideal weight, each additional pound costs you a month of your life. In fact, to get an idea of what being overweight does to your health, consider the following figures:

For people who are overweight by:	The increase in the death rate is:
10%	13%
20%	25%
30%	40%

An overweight condition is also associated with an increased incidence of coronary artery disease, it often leads to high blood pressure, and it places a definite burden on the heart: the heart must work harder because every activity is more difficult for a heavy person.

The value of losing weight is tremendous:

- Hypertensive patients oftentimes have a significant improvement in their blood pressures.
- Blood fats—triglycerides—tend to return toward normal.
- Diabetics have less trouble handling sugar loads.
- Most important, you tend to feel better, feel less tired, and have a better self-image.

It's important to understand that virtually everyone can lose weight. Many people erroneously think the opposite, but being overweight seldom is due to familial or inherited factors or to "abnormal metabolism." Being overweight is simply the result of bad habits. It comes down to eating too much and being too inactive.

Tip-the-Scale Tips

How are you going to get those excess pounds off? There are literally hundreds of books written about dieting, and a great number of them aren't very good. While we do not plan to go into any of the programs, we will say this: There is no sense going on a crash diet every three months. It probably does more harm than good. Diet pills aren't of any value either. There aren't any temporary measures. You have to watch what you eat on a *continuing* basis and cut down on those calories.

If you really want to take weight off or watch your weight, here are some ways to do it:

- *Skip* junk foods and those foods that add calories without offering many vitamins or minerals—for example, extra cocktails, fats, sugar and sugary foods such as canned fruits, soft drinks, sugar-coated breakfast cereals, honey, syrups, or rich desserts such as cakes and ice cream.

- *Substitute* more nutritious, less fattening foods than those you have been eating—for example, fish and poultry, fruits and fruit juices, vegetables, clear soups, low-calorie beverages, nonfat milk. Foods having naturally occurring sugars, complex carbohydrates, such as fruits, vegetables, peas, green beans, some starches, cereals, and whole grains (including whole wheat bread) are nutritious, full of vitamins and minerals, low in saturated fat and calories. Fruits and vegetables also have a type of fiber that helps lower cholesterol, and foods with wheat and bran contain another fiber that may prevent bowel cancer.

- *Cut down* on the size of the portions you eat—and eat more slowly (you don't stay hungry that way).

- *Shop more carefully.* Don't shop when you're hungry. You tend to buy everything you see. Everyone tends to eat what they have in the house.

- *Exercise.* It probably takes only 15 to 30 minutes a day of exercise to counteract some of those excess calories you've been taking in.

Of course, the key to all this is you have to *want* to control your weight. You have to be motivated. You have to want to break those bad eating habits. And in order to come to grips with those emotionally charged situations that lead to your eating or snacking, you must understand them and cope with them.

These are the general approaches. You can also count those calories more carefully. The table on the next page shows how many calories you should be taking in each day once you reach your ideal weight. Appendix G gives you the details of the calorie content of various foods, and Appendix H the calories expended in various physical activities.

Right now it may seem like an overwhelming undertaking to change that old body of yours. But thousands of people have learned to control their weight without much difficulty, simply because over the years they've knowingly or unknowingly developed many of the habits suggested above. Try some of them. You'll love that new wardrobe.

Calorie Allowance for Adults
of Average Physical Activity

DESIRABLE WEIGHT	25 YEARS	45 YEARS	65 YEARS
Men			
110	2300	2050	1750
120	2400	2200	1850
130	2550	2300	1950
140	2700	2450	2050
150	2850	2550	2150
160	3000	2700	2250
170	3100	2800	2350
180	3250	2950	2450
190	3400	3050	2600
Women			
90	1600	1500	1250
100	1750	1600	1350
110	1900	1700	1450
120	2000	1800	1500
130	2100	1900	1600
140	2250	2050	1700
150	2350	2150	1800
160	2500	2250	1900

Source: U.S. Department of Agriculture.

CHAPTER 17

Drinking: One Martini, Two Martini, Three Martini, Four . . .

Bᴇᴛ you're afraid we're going to tell you to stop drinking.

We're not.

By and large, alcohol is not a risk factor; it is not known to lead to coronary disease. However, as long as we're talking about putting things in your mouth, as we have in the last two chapters, it is appropriate to talk about alcohol also.

Alcohol isn't dangerous after a heart attack when it is consumed in moderation—that is, 2 to 4 ounces per day. It may be necessary to restrict your intake, however, if you have a high triglyceride level or a weight problem. In addition, you should watch the drinking before and during exercise, since alcohol dilates blood vessels, and this may result in your feeling faint while exercising.

Of course, excessive drinking and alcohol abuse is a serious problem, not only in the United States but all over the world. If you think you might be in this category of drinker, you should be aware that excessive amounts of alcohol over long periods of time may injure not only your liver but also your heart. For the average person who has angina pectoris or who has had a heart attack, however, one or two cocktails before dinner, or wine with dinner, or even an after-dinner drink can be enjoyed without risk.

CHAPTER **18**

Exercise: Lifting a Finger to Help Yourself

Exercise. An unpleasant word to a lot of people.

Exercise means *effort*—either boring, repetitive effort ("What kind of fun is running around an oval track?") or stressful, threatening effort ("At my age and weight, how can I get out on a tennis court with all those young folks watching me?").

O.K., but how would you like your doctor to prescribe a pill that makes you:

• Less tired, anxious, and stressed.
• Feel more confident.
• Look more handsome and attractive.

That's what exercise does.

It may even help you avoid repeating the frightening coronary you have just had, though no one is certain of this. In addition, an exercise program helps bring down the blood triglycerides when they're elevated and increases another fat called HDL which may actually *protect* against the progress of coronary disease, according to a new (albeit unproved) theory.

One thing, unfortunately, that exercise does *not* do: it does not stimulate the growth of new coronary arteries, of collateral vessels. Medical scientists had believed previously that it might do so, but this hasn't panned out in recent research.

But exercise, it has been philosophized, is the closest thing there is to an antiaging pill. And for heart patients in particular, exercise can help condition the heart so it works as efficiently as it is capable (indeed, some former heart patients have even become marathon runners—though we're not going to guarantee this in your case, or even suggest you try), as well as tone up other muscles, help you control your weight, control high blood pressure and diabetes, get back to work quicker, and help you return to a normal life.

And it need not be boring or threatening.

Exercise Testing

Of course you can't just put on sneakers and get out there. Perhaps more than any other area (except medication) this is where you have to work closely with your doctor.

First of all, he or she may ask you to take an exercise test or so-called *treadmill test* or stress EKG ("stress" doesn't mean worry here; it means effort on the heart). Exercise testing is used for many things. It is used to test people who haven't had heart attacks but have been inactive and want to start exercising again. It is used to diagnose coronary disease, to distinguish other conditions that might present similar symptoms, and to evaluate the severity of coronary disease. Finally, it's also used to follow the progress of patients who have had coronary bypass surgery. Many people do not need an exercise test; that's up to the physician.

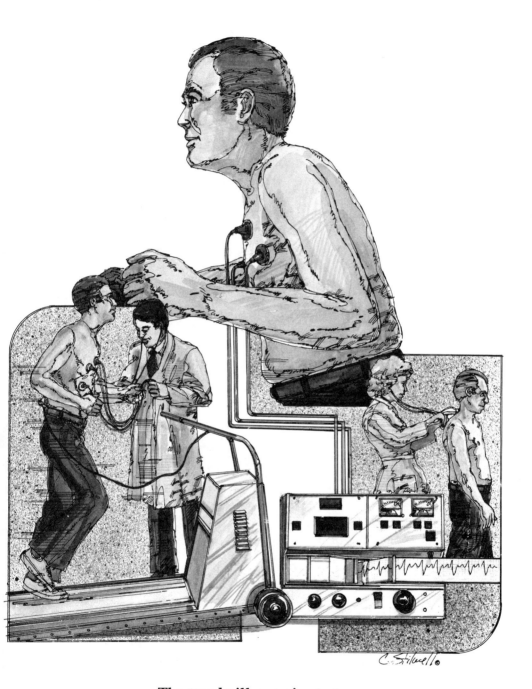

The treadmill exercise test

In the treadmill test, you will have the same sort of electrocardiogram taken that we described earlier, only you will be required to have it done while walking or running on a motor-driven treadmill or while pedaling a stationary bicycle. Your heart needs to get more blood during exercise because it is working harder, and if it doesn't get a sufficient blood supply, certain changes often show up on the electrocardiogram. At the start of the test, the amount of exercise required is slight (a slow saunter), but as it continues, you will exercise more and more, perhaps reaching a run. From this, the physician can see how well your heart responds to a work load by analyzing your electrocardiogram and the heart-rate and blood-pressure changes.

If you are having this test within the first month after a heart attack, much less exercise will be required than four, six, or twelve months later. You'll probably not even be asked to run but rather to walk somewhat briskly.

In addition, your doctor may want you to undergo the treadmill test using small quantities of radioactive substances called *radioisotopes,* which are injected into your bloodstream in order to identify areas of the heart where the delivery of blood may be insufficient. (Don't worry, this is a very low and safe amount of radioactivity, far less than those in x-rays, for example.)

The purpose of all this is, of course, simply to determine the range of reasonable limits of exercise: too little may weaken you; too much might be dangerous. The test in effect helps your doctor design an exercise prescription for you to follow.

Easing into Exercise

It is terribly important that you start your exercise program *slowly,* despite the inclination to try and undo perhaps years of inactivity with a lot of hard activity. Starting too vigorously is not only dangerous but will give you sore muscles and joints, which can only discourage you from further exercise.

One of the main goals during an exercise program is progressively to increase your heart rate. As we will see, you will be asked to achieve what are called *target heart rates*. During the early stages, while you are still in the hospital, the target heart rate that you initially reach will be up to only 100 or 110 beats per minute (for periods of 5 to 10 minutes at first). At home and as the months pass, your heart rate will be allowed to go to 120 to 130, then 130 to 150 beats per minute. Whatever your rate of progress, the program will be individually tailored for you by your physician.

The way to monitor your heart rate is to take your pulse. You should learn to do this yourself, so that you

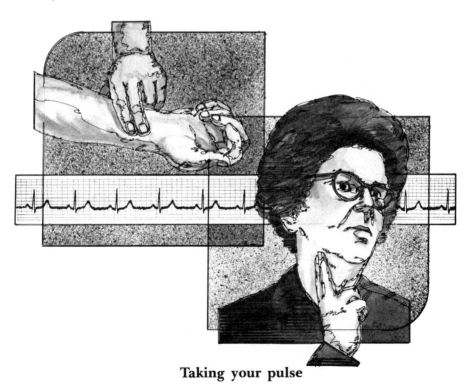

Taking your pulse

can tell when you have reached your reasonable limits of physical activity. Taking a pulse is easy and can be learned from your doctor or nurse in a few minutes. A pulse can be taken on a wrist (with index and middle finger), on the neck, or (if you're not shy) in the groin. You'll need a watch with a second hand. Count the number of pulses that occur in a half minute, and multiply by 2 to get your heartbeats per minute.

Exercise Tips

As we noted in Chapter 2, you will already have started exercising in the hospital, with the help of a nurse or physical therapist. Here we are concerned about easing you into exercise after you get home.

SOME DON'TS:

- Don't strain against or lift heavy objects.
- Don't do sudden or rapid activity, such as fast running.
- On the other hand, don't do stationary exercise (isometric exercise), in which the muscles are tightly flexed but there is no movement.
- Don't exercise if you feel unusually fatigued or ill.
- Don't take hot or cold showers or baths before and after exercise. They may lead to a fall in blood pressure or irregular heartbeat. (Moderately warm water is O.K.)
- Don't drink alcohol for an hour before and after exercise.
- Don't get into heavy competitive games.

SOME DO'S:

- Do *warm up* for 5 to 10 minutes before the exercise session with light calisthenics, including stretching, twisting, touching toes, bending at the waist, bending knees and elbows, or otherwise moving the limbs (but avoid

Warm up

Exercise

Cool down

straining). Warming up not only limbers you and so prevents bone, muscle, and joint injuries; it also protects your heart against unnecessary stress, since you are beginning gradually.

- Do *cool down* for 3 to 5 minutes after exercise, gradually diminishing but not stopping the exercise. This prevents large amounts of blood from "pooling" in the legs, which can cause dizziness and even fainting.
- Do start exercising on level ground, avoiding hills. It's a good idea to begin any jogging on a soft surface such as grass or a cinder track to avoid the injuries that can occur when running on a hard street or sidewalk. Once you get used to exercise, you can move on to these harder surfaces. Proper running shoes also prevent a lot of aches and pains.
- Do exercise at least 3 to 4 times a week. Every single day is not necessary, though.
- Do ask your doctor about exercising at (or traveling to) places at high altitudes. Most heart-attack patients can tolerate elevations between 3,500 and 6,000 feet well, but some people are troubled by angina or shortness of breath at these altitudes. In any event, remember that any type of exercise takes more energy at these higher elevations, so you should exercise less than you normally do, especially the first day or so while you're becoming acclimatized.

Danger Zone

Be aware of the following *danger signs* while you are exercising. If any of them happen, consult your doctor.

- Severe or unusual fatigue.
- Dizziness or fainting during or after exercise.
- Unusually heavy perspiration.
- Irregular or unusually rapid heartbeat.

- Unusual shortness of breath (especially if it prevents you from speaking after you have stopped the exercise).
- Your heart rate does not return to normal within 10 minutes after exercise is over.
- New chest pain or pain that remains after you stop. (If you're taking nitroglycerin tablets, and 3 or 4 tablets and 15 minutes of rest do not make the pain go away, see your physician immediately.)

Your Exercise Program

As we stated, your precise exercise program will be worked out between you and your doctor. Remember, though, that the two things to watch for are:

- *Your target heart rate*—which you monitor by taking your pulse. The aim of all exercise programs is to *gradually* increase the work load on the heart—that is, gradually over a period of time, increase the target heart rate.
- *Potential danger*–excessive fatigue, chest pain, shortness of breath, irregular heart rate.

On the next three pages are three exercise programs that your doctor may prescribe or modify. If they seem boring or threatening, talk it out with him or her. Perhaps some modifications can be made. Remember that a good exercise program gradually *increases the degree and duration of activity* over a period of days, weeks, and months.

PROGRAM #1: LIGHT CONDITIONING. This is for the first 2 to 8 weeks following a heart attack, and involves leisurely and then more brisk *walking*. Some persons, particularly the elderly, may not want to proceed beyond this program. You start by walking leisurely for 10 to 20 minutes, and by the third or fourth week for longer periods of 30 to 40 minutes.

After the fourth week, the exercise is divided into segments of 5-minute periods of leisurely walking and 5-minute periods of slightly more brisk walking, in which you try to achieve target heart rates of 110 to 115 beats per minute during the brisker periods. This is done at first for 30 to 40 minutes, and by the fifth to sixth weeks, for 40 to 50 minutes.

Finally, between the sixth and eighth weeks, you should be walking the entire 45- to 50-minute periods at a brisk pace, maintaining the target heart rate of 110 to 115 beats per minute. Rate of speed is more important than distance traveled in this exercise. The approximate distances during each of these stages are shown in the table.

Exercise Program #1: Light Conditioning

TIME AFTER HEART ATTACK (WEEKS)	TYPE OF EXERCISE	DURATION OF EXERCISE (MINUTES)	APPROXIMATE DISTANCE (MILES)
2–3	Leisurely walk	10–20	½–¾
3–4	Leisurely walk	30–40	¾–1¼
4–5	Alternate 5 min. each leisurely and brisk walking. Target heart rates: under 110 (leisurely), 110–115 (brisk)	30–40	1¼–1½
5–6	Alternate 5 min. each leisurely and brisk walking. Target heart rates: under 110 (leisurely) 110–115 (brisk)	40–50	1½–2
6–8	Brisk walking only. Target heart rates: 110–115	45–50	2½–4
8	Begin Exercise Program #2, or continue with 6–8 week program.		

PROGRAM #2: ACTIVE CONDITIONING.   Begun 8 weeks after a
heart attack, this program combines walking and jogging
30 to 45 minutes three or more times a week. You begin
by *jogging* 30 paces and *walking* 60 paces, continuing for
about 30 minutes, during which you achieve a target
heart rate of approximately 130 beats per minute while
jogging, slowing down to 110 beats per minute or less
while walking. As the months go by, the duration of exercise is lengthened, as the amount of jogging is increased
and the period that you walk is decreased. At the same
time, the target heart rate goes up, so that, for example,
at 2½ to 4 months, a target heart rate of 130 to 150 is
reached while jogging, slowing to 130 or below while
walking. After the first six months, jogging occupies the
entire exercise period, reaching target rates of 135 to
155, the exercise periods lasting 30 to 45 minutes.

Exercise Program #2: Active Conditioning

TIME AFTER HEART ATTACK (MONTHS)	PACES WALKED	HEART RATE	PACES JOGGED	TARGET HEART RATE	TOTAL DURATION (MINUTES)
2–2¼	60	110	30	130	30
2¼–2½	30	110	30	130	30
2½–3	60	120	60	130	30
3–4	60	120	90	150	30–40
4–5	60	130	120	150	30–40
5–6	60	130	180	150	30–40
Over 6			All jogged	155	30–45

PROGRAM #3: ALTERNATIVE ACTIVE CONDITIONING. If you find walking and jogging too boring, this program, which also begins 8 weeks after a heart attack, permits swimming or riding a regular or stationary bicycle, if your doctor approves.

Exercise Program #3: Alternative Active Conditioning

TIME AFTER HEART ATTACK (MONTHS)	DURATION OF SLOW EXERCISE (MINUTES)	DURATION OF BRISK EXERCISE (MINUTES)	TARGET HEART RATE (FOR BRISK EXERCISE)	TOTAL DURATION (MINUTES)
2–2½	1	½	130	30
2½–3	1	1	130	30
3–4	1	1½	150	30–40
4–5	1	2	150	30–40
5–6	1	3	150	30–40
Over 6	1	3	155	30–40

Other Activities: Support the METs

As your heart gets stronger and you develop more endurance, you may want to switch to other kinds of activity—again, if your physician approves. One way to evaluate other forms of activity is to see what their energy cost is. These are expressed as *MET values,* which have nothing to do with a New York baseball team but are multiples of the amount of energy that you are using while just resting. The MET values of different kinds of activities are given in Appendix I.

If you plan to take up activities that are going to require more than minimal amount of strain on your *arms,* you may also want to begin exercising them. At first try simple calisthenics, the flexing and stretching exercises we discussed. Then, over the next few weeks, practice lifting light objects, such as canned goods, raising them above your head and out to the side or in front of you with your arms extended. Start by lifting them five times; as you get stronger, you may lift them 10, 15, and eventually 20 times.

For exercise to do its job, you must do it at least three times a week—indefinitely. Make sure, therefore, that it isn't boring or threatening. Make sure it's fun.

CHAPTER **19**

Take Your Medicine

AMERICANS have taken so many over-the-counter and prescription drugs over the years that they have become accustomed to them as part of their daily lives. As a result, they frequently fail to respect fully the danger of using potent drugs or medications, which have the potential for doing harm as well as good unless they are used properly.

Your Medication Guide

Here are ten simple but important tips to make sure your medicines work for you and not against you.

• *Learn the names of the medications you are taking and do your best to understand why you are taking them.* That doesn't mean that you should second-guess your physician or try to acquire an instant medical education. It does mean, however, that you should be as informed as possible about what you are putting into your body.

- *Take medications in the amounts and at the times ordered by
your physician.* Some patients have a tendency to modify
the dosage of medications prescribed, which can have
serious consequences. Your body normally is an orderly
and highly complex system, and an improper dosage of
some drugs can lead to certain physical changes you
may find difficult to tolerate. Taking more medication
than the amount your physician ordered may not only
be less effective, it may be dangerous. Skipping doses
can be equally bad. It is particularly hazardous when
you attempt to catch up with missed doses by doubling
up on future doses. Remember that, most of the time,
you are the most essential element in the treatment, because *you* administer the remedy.

- *Don't stop taking a medication that has been prescribed for you
without first consulting your physician about it.* Some drugs
are most effective only when the series of dosage is
completed. Others may do more harm than good if
they are stopped prematurely or suddenly. Don't fall
into the subtle trap of stopping "by accident" because
your supply ran out and you failed to have it refilled.

- *Check with your physician before taking any medications,
whether prescribed or not.* Certain drugs interact with one
another. The result can be that they interfere with each
other or increase the reaction you may have to each of
them. The consequences may be far different from
what you anticipated. Even over-the-counter drug preparations such as aspirin and cold remedies contain
chemicals that sometimes can be harmful when taken
under some conditions, and they may react adversely
with prescription medications you are taking.

- *Don't take medications prescribed for someone else.* A physician prescribes *individually,* for the unique conditions
found in *each* patient. Since we're all different, each of
us may react differently to the same medication.

- *Be sure to contact your physician if you have any reaction to a
medication you did not anticipate.* Every drug has a large

number of possible side effects—and they may be some you can't tolerate.

- *Keep all medications out of the reach of small children.* Some children are attracted to the bright colors or the smell and taste. They also often imitate what they see adults do, and will try to take your medicine.

- *If you have any medication more than several months old, ask your pharmacist if it is still safe and effective to use. And throw out any drug that has been in your medicine chest more than two years without being used.* Some medications become ineffective or even harmful as they become older.

- *Keep each medicine in its own labeled container.* Under no circumstances should any liquid medicine or pills be put into a bottle or pillbox that contains other medicines. Such an act, which may be intended as a measure of economy, may end in tragedy.

- *Bring all of your medications with you when you visit your physician.* It is usually the best way to identify what you have been taking. Many pills are the same shape and color, and that similarity may make it difficult for you to describe accurately the prescriptions that you have at home.

Side Effects

Any drug has the potential for causing a wide range of unwanted side effects. Aspirin, for instance, is responsible for more than 20 of them.

Side effects to various drugs may include:

- Allergic reactions—fever, rash, aching joints, yellow skin, swelling of hands or face, or difficult breathing.

- Nausea, vomiting, or diarrhea.

- Fatigue.

- Anemia.

	MON		TUE		WED		THUR		FRI		SAT		SUN	
	AM	PM	AM	PM	AM	PM	AM	PM	AM	PM	AM	PM	AM	PM
Drug: Digoxin **Amount:** 0.25 mg./pill **Dosage:** 1 pill each day	8		8		8		8		8		8		8	
Drug: Hydrochlorothiazide **Amount:** 50 mg./pill **Dosage:** 1 pill twice a day	8	5	8	5	8	5	8	5	8	5	8	5	8	5
Drug: Potassium Chloride **Amount:** 20 mEq. / 1 tsp. **Dosage:** 1 tsp twice a day	8	5	8	5	8	5	8	5	8	5	8	5	8	5
Drug: Coumadin **Amount:** 5 mg./pill **Dosage:** 1 pill every other day	8				8				8				8	

Drug calendar

Some side effects are mild and can be ignored. Some
are disturbing and cause discomfort but usually can be
controlled or relieved by a change in dosage of the medication taken or a change of the medication itself. Other
side effects are potentially dangerous, requiring that your
physician be notified. Some of the more common side effects to cardiovascular drugs are given in Appendix A.

Helping You to Help Yourself

While you are still in the hospital, your physician, nurse,
or other member of the health recovery team will tell
you:

- The name of the medication you are taking.
- How to tell it apart from other medications.
- The reason your physician prescribed it.
- Some of its side effects.
- Any special precautions you should use.

As you prepare for discharge from the hospital, you
will again be instructed in the identifying characteristics
(such as color, size, and shape) and use of the drugs prescribed for you. You may decide to keep a drug calendar
such as the one on the opposite page, in order to help
keep track of your drugs. Read Appendix A for more
details about these medications. It is essential to your recovery and comfort that you understand everything you
can about them.

CHAPTER 20

Your Sex Life

Do you have to stop having sex? Of course not. In fact, it is *desirable* to resume your usual sex life: mutually loving relationships are extremely important, and particularly so following a heart attack.

Isn't there some danger? Not if you're careful. Sex is, after all, a form of mild to moderate physical activity. The stress on the cardiovascular system and increased blood pressure, heart rate, and respiration rate during sex is no more than that of climbing a couple of flights of stairs. While some people may suffer a bit of anginal chest pain during sex, it is usually rapidly alleviated with immediate rest and, occasionally, a nitroglycerin tablet. You simply should not be timid about going back to your usual sex life.

As you might expect, the most frequent question patients ask about sex is: When can I resume? This is up to your physician, who knows how severe your heart injury was. You should not begin an active sex life without first discussing it with your doctor. In most cases, however, sex can be resumed in 3 to 6 weeks after the heart attack.

The Joy of Sex

Here are some suggestions that help you resume a satisfying sex life:

- A loving and considerate act of love should take place in a calm and serene atmosphere. Avoid arguments or emotional discussions that cause you or your partner unnecessary excitement or anxiety. If there were any unresolved tensions associated with sex before your heart attack, they will probably continue to be a problem, and you should not feel reluctant about seeking psychological counseling. Either partner may become fearful of having sex—fear either of the activity itself or the accompanying excitement. These emotions are often needlessly exaggerated. Open communication between the two of you goes a long way toward dealing with these anxieties.

- Find positions comfortable for both of you. Sex need not involve gymnastics to be satisfying. Alternate the customary male-female positions, or have no hesitancy about following sexual preferences that you and your partner find mutually comfortable, if it proves easier.

- Avoid having sex when you are unduly fatigued.

- Avoid having sex immediately after eating a meal, since the digestive system will be making heavy demands on the blood supply, and the additional demand required during sexual activity may place the heart under unusual strain.

- Avoid sex in locations or in weather when it is very hot or very cold, since your cardiovascular system will already be under the stress of controlling your body's temperature.

- Avoid drinking a lot of alcohol before sex. A small amount may help relax you, but large amounts will dilate the blood vessels, causing an increase in the heart rate, which means the heart has to work harder.

- Some drugs such as tranquilizers or those used to control high blood pressure may interfere with sexual performance. If they do, call your physician. An adjustment in the amount, type, or time of taking the medication may be all that is required.

Sex is, of course, a form of physical exercise. Thus, the better your physical fitness and muscle tone, the less strain on your cardiovascular system.

Caveats

If you sometimes feel anginal chest pain during sex, here's what to do:

- Take one or two nitroglycerin tablets *before* you begin to become aroused.
- Take nitroglycerin tablets to relieve chest pain developing during the sexual activity. Don't take more than a total of three over a short period of time. (If you need more, that means you need to see a physician.)
- Rest for 15 to 30 minutes before resuming sexual activity.

You should seek medical attention when:

- The angina pain remains unrelieved after you've taken three or more nitroglycerin tablets.
- Rest and inactivity does not relieve the pain.
- You feel a higher than normal heartbeat rate or irregular heart rhythm.
- Sweating lasts more than 15 minutes after orgasm.

Don't let this list of cautions deter you from beginning to reactivate your sex life. We all need love, in sickness and in health—and so does your partner.

CHAPTER **21**

Going Back to Work

O_{NE} of the most frequently asked questions we hear is, "When can I go back to work?" You will be very pleased to learn that about 85 percent of patients with uncomplicated myocardial infarction sooner or later return to work.

Most return within the first 6 weeks to 3 months, but it is not unusual to take longer. Just when you go back is a decision to be worked out between you and your doctor. Here are some of the factors that will enter into the decision:

- The severity of your heart attack and how much heart muscle is damaged.
- The speed of your recovery. Although, as might be expected, older people take longer to bounce back than younger ones, recovery is still an individual matter. A lot depends, of course, on what kind of shape you were in before the heart attack.
- How hard you work to make yourself healthy again— whether you lose weight, get to exercising, and so on.

- The kind of job you hold—for example, desk work versus heavy-labor job.

Simulation

After 3 to 6 weeks as your recovery proceeds, it's a good idea to *simulate* your work activity at home. If you have a desk job involving lots of decisions and interruptions and phone calls, set up a situation with a co-worker in which you are called with questions from time to time throughout the day (start this gradually, of course—we don't want you tense about day-to-day problems on the job when you're only just out of the hospital). If you're in more of a manufacturing or laboring occupation, see if you can set up some shop or gardening activity that approximates what you do. (Or, under the watchful eye of your doctor, you might get a treadmill test.) The idea of all this is to see whether the work is going to bother you.

Some types of jobs permit employees to go back part time. If this is so in your field, by all means do it this way. If you cannot, then don't try to jump the gun—wait until your physician says it's O.K.

In some cases, where the job is an unusually strenuous one, or if you remain very ill, it may be best to face the facts and consider changing jobs—or even changing occupations. Look under "Vocational Consultants" in the Yellow Pages of the phone book, or call your city or county social services department for a recommendation on a vocational counselor, if it seems like this might be the best choice for you. Discuss it with your doctor.

Money

The real question behind the question as to when one can return to work is, in most cases, a question about money. Few of us feel we can go without working for long because few of us have the wherewithal to go a long time without income and not have a reduced standard of living.

If you feel this might be the case, don't sit around worrying about it. Get some advice. Get your spouse or a friend researching your job benefits. Have someone look into workman's compensation. See what insurance policies apply. If you have an accountant or a lawyer, take up the matter with him or her. Don't let yourself get into an emotional funk about it. As we said earlier in the book, the best attitude to take in your recovery is (1) acceptance, and (2) a positive outlook.

Driving

As a footnote to the subject of returning to work, we should say something about driving. When will you be able to resume driving a car again? This is a tricky question that can only be answered by your physician. Most driving is not taxing and can be resumed in 3 to 4 weeks. However, in heavy traffic, driving can produce increased heart rates, and your doctor may advise you to wait awhile before undertaking this kind of driving again. Some states require a physician's approval before a person can return to driving after a heart attack.

The main point to keep in mind is that most people return to productive employment after their heart attack and are able to continue working for years to come.

CHAPTER **22**

Recovery for Older People

IF it somehow seems like we've been talking to the under-65s in this book (as in the preceding chapter on going back to work), we do not mean that to be the case. The book is for everyone.

Now, it is true that people age in different ways, and many people in their seventies and over are "younger"—more alive, alert, and active—than people half their age, and so are apt to recover from a heart attack as effectively as any younger person. Even so, there are some special considerations to be aware of if you or someone you know is a heart patient over 70.

The Recovery Period

Because in older people many things heal more slowly (even a cut finger) and because the heart has less overall reserve capacity, and thus is somewhat less able to withstand the damage caused by a heart attack, the recovery period consequently may be longer—perhaps several weeks or months longer. In addition, many elderly people

may suffer from a variety of other illnesses present before the attack, and these too may affect recovery time.

Yet, at the same time, there is probably less need to
return to a highly active life. Few people in their late seventies work at a full-time job. Many at that age are happy
to spend their time with their retirement interests and
with their family and friends.

After the patient has left the hospital and is re-
cuperating at home, it's generally a good idea to be sure
he or she is not left alone or not left alone with a spouse
or friend who is also ill.

Some older people may have vision problems, so that
they find it difficult to read medication and other instructions, or they may have failings of memory so that they
forget to take their medicines.

To help with medical problems and with the general
running of the household, the patient should be provided
with care by family members, live-in help, or members of
the local visiting nurses' association. Family members in
particular should learn as much as they can about heart
attacks and coronary disease.

Therapy

Because elderly people tend to be less flexible, less able to
change time-worn habits, family members and physicians
are advised to take a less-rigid line and settle for com-
promises rather than insist the patient follow every instruction exactly. Though medications should be taken
precisely as prescribed, everything else we have discussed
in this book—diet modifications, exercise programs, even
stopping smoking—are less important. (However, if severe high blood pressure or congestive heart failure are
present, it may be important to follow a low-salt diet.)

Of course, the patient should be encouraged to be as
active as possible, but a structured exercise program may
not be possible, especially if the patient is confined to bed,

or even desirable, since there are the dangers of falling and fracturing a bone. However, every elderly patient, to the extent possible, should be encouraged to get up and move about to some degree.

Medication can pose a problem, not only because elderly patients may have vision and memory difficulties, but also because they seem to be somewhat less tolerant of medications and are more likely to develop undesirable side effects. For example, nitroglycerin may produce a marked fall in blood pressure in older people and so should be administered very carefully. After taking nitroglycerin, an elderly person should not stand up suddenly within the first 5 minutes.

Digitalis may also produce more undesirable reactions in older persons, and a patient and his or her family should be very aware of the potential side effects (see Chapter 19 and Appendix A), so that the warning signs will be recognized should they appear.

Although it is true that recovery may be less than complete in an older coronary patient, this does not mean that one cannot come back to a happy, active, productive life. Indeed, in many cases the quality of life can be better than it was before.

CHAPTER **23**

Heart Clubs

T HIS may be the shortest chapter in the book, but it's an important one. Its message is: You are not alone. As we stated earlier, nearly a million and a half people suffer heart attacks every year and an additional 100,000 or more have strokes.

Many of these people have gotten together in heart clubs organized either by health professionals or by patients themselves. Just as groups of people like yourself can often help you in quitting smoking or losing weight, so other heart patients can help you in understanding what you should or should not do, assist you in starting an exercise program and retooling your eating habits, and answering questions you have. Thus, when we're asked whether it's worth looking into heart clubs, our answer is: Yes. In spades.

Ask the staff at your hospital about them. Or call your local heart association.

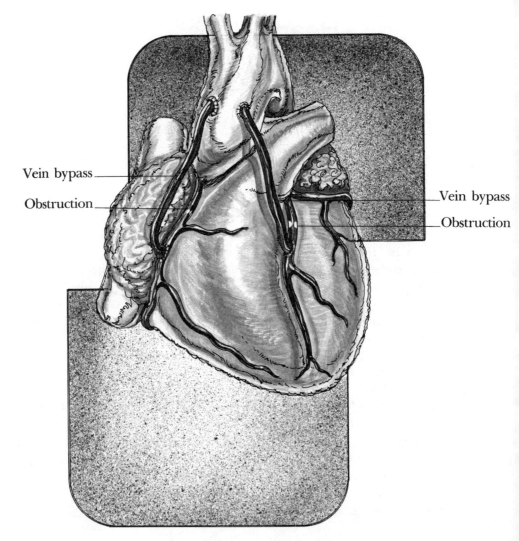

Vein bypass

Obstruction

Vein bypass

Obstruction

Coronary artery bypass

CHAPTER 24

Coronary Bypass Surgery and Coronary Angiography

I⊤ is amazing the number of people who have had heart and coronary problems who ask us about the subject of bypass surgery—even though for most there is little chance they would be candidates for it. Nevertheless, it is an important and fascinating subject, so let's describe it here.

In some cases, the best way to keep an adequate supply of blood flowing into the heart is to surgically implant more blood vessels to act as additional coronary arteries. This procedure is called *coronary bypass surgery* or *aortocoronary (AC) bypass surgery.*

Most patients with angina pectoris or who have suffered heart attacks can be treated perfectly well without this operation. However, it is recommended for patients with worsening or severe angina that does not improve with standard medication and for some patients with very severe coronary disease who are threatened by the possibility of a serious heart attack.

The first bypass operation was performed in 1964, and by now upwards of 300,000 procedures have been performed in the United States. It is a relatively safe procedure, with a 95 percent or greater chance of one's getting through the operation successfully. If disabling angina is present, there is a better than 75 percent likelihood that the pain will be diminished or eliminated. The surgery may also prolong lives of some patients with narrowing of particularly critical areas of the coronary system.

However, despite such gratifying results, the procedure will not *necessarily* eliminate angina pain in all patients or prevent heart attacks from occurring, and will not delay the progression of atherosclerosis. Even after 15 years of experience, there is still a great deal to be learned about the results of such operations.

The decision as to whether you should have bypass surgery should never be made lightly. A number of questions should be considered by you, your family, and physician together, among them:

• How old are you?

• How able are you to work or live the kind of life you desire?

• How incapacitating is the angina?

• Are symptoms progressive?

• How well do you respond to medications?

• What are the results of your exercise tests?

• What is the severity of coronary narrowing?

In addition to these factors, you and your doctor must weigh the potential *benefits* of the operation against the *risks* of surgery.

Coronary Angiography

Before bypass surgery can be considered, a specific test must be performed called *coronary angiography* (or "coronary arteriography," "a coronary arteriogram"). This test involves the injection of a special dye into the coronary arteries. The dye can be seen on x-ray film as it flows through the arteries, and thus any obstruction of the coronary arteries can be seen and the location and severity of narrowing can be pinpointed.

The test is usually done in the hospital. An area of the groin or arm is numbed with a local anesthetic (such as novocaine). One of the blood vessels passing through the arm or groin is entered by a needle or tiny incision, and a thin, long tube (a catheter) is passed through this vessel to an area just outside the heart, where its tip is directed into the openings of the coronary arteries. Then the dye is injected into the arteries, x-ray movies or still shots are taken, and the films are analyzed to locate regions of narrowing within the coronary arteries.

How the Bypass Operation Is Done

If it is decided to proceed with bypass surgery, the patient is put to sleep with a general anesthetic. While the operation is in progress, a life-support system called a *heart-lung machine* is connected to the patient's circulatory system, to temporarily relieve the heart and lungs of their normal function while the heart is being worked on. This is called *open-heart surgery*, and it is used in other cardiac conditions such as diseased valves or when there are congenital holes in the heart.

The operation is accomplished by taking a piece of vein from the patient's leg (occasionally an artery from the inner chest is used) and securing it from the aorta to a portion of coronary artery beyond the point of obstruction. This way, it is used to *bypass* (detour) blood around the area of the blocked artery.

Other Operations in Coronary Disease

After some serious heart attacks, a pouch or bulge forms on the left ventricular muscle called a *ventricular aneurysm*. Most of these produce no problems, but if they are very large, they can cause congestive failure or rhythm disturbances. In such instances, it may be necessary to surgically excise the aneurysm—a procedure called *ventricular aneurysmectomy*.

In other cases, the mitral valve may develop a leak after a heart attack. Most of the time the leak is very slight and produces no problems whatever, but in rare cases an excessive amount of blood may leak through the valve, congestive failure may develop, and the valve may need to be replaced surgically.

There are now a great number of artificial (prosthetic) valves available for replacement. Some are made out of cloth, metal and plastic (the so-called *ball valves,* for example) and some are actually made partly from the heart valves of pigs. These tissue valves are "cured"— meaning they are not alive—and therefore aren't rejected, as may happen in heart transplantation. The pig-tissue valves are mounted on a cloth-covered ring that can be sewn in place.

When performed on carefully selected patients, bypass grafting and the other operations are extremely useful therapy. However, again it must be stressed that most people with heart attacks or angina do admirably well without surgery.

EPILOGUE

The Days Ahead

W E could have called this book *Ten Easy Steps to Recovering from Your Heart Attack* and maybe retired on the royalties.

But the title would not be honest. There are no easy steps to coming back. Yet the experience of millions shows that it is possible, and we're sure it's possible for you.

Now you know the basics. What follows—the bibliography, the glossary, the detailed appendixes—are intended as further explorations. There's a lot you can do—not just to recover but to expand the quality of your life.

This is not the end. It is the beginning.

BIBLIOGRAPHY

Other Books to Help You

Health and Medicine

Judith K. Jones, *The Good Housekeeping Guide to Medicine and Drugs.* New York: Hearst Books, 1977.

Donald M. Vickery and James F. Fries, *Take Care of Yourself: A Consumer's Guide to Medical Care.* Reading, Mass.: Addison-Wesley Publishing Company, 1976.

Smoking

O. F. Pomerleau and C. S. Pomerleau, *Break the Smoking Habit.* Champaign, Ill.: Research Press, 1977.

The Smoke Watchers' How-to-Quit Book. New York: Bernard Geis Associates, 1970.

Smoking Self-Testing Kit. National Clearing House for Smoking and Health, 5401 Westlund Ave., Bethesda, Md. 20016.

Stress

Herbert Benson, *The Relaxation Response.* New York: William Morrow and Company, 1975.

C. Eugene Walker, *Learn to Relax: 13 Ways to Reduce Tension.* Englewood Cliffs, N.J.: Prentice-Hall, 1975.

Low Cholesterol and Low Saturated Fat Cooking

Ruth Eshleman and Mary Winston, *The American Heart Association Cookbook*. New York: David McKay Co., 1975.

Kay B. Heiss and C. Gordon Heiss, *Eat to Your Heart's Content: The Low Cholesterol Gourmet Cookbook*. San Francisco: Chronicle Books, 1972.

Alan Hooker, *Herb Cookery*. San Francisco: 101 Productions, 1971.

Helen Cassidy Page and John Speer Schroeder, *The Whole Family Low Cholesterol Cookbook*. New York: Grosset & Dunlap, 1976.

Weight Control

William E. Connor, Sonja L. Connor, Martha M. Fry, and Susan L. Warner, *The Alternative Diet Book*. Iowa City, Iowa: Department of Publications and Printing Service, University of Iowa, 1976.

Michael J. Mahoney and Kathryn Mahoney, *Permanent Weight Control: A Total Solution to the Dieter's Dilemma*. New York: W. W. Norton, 1976.

Jean Nidetch, *Weight Watchers International Cookbook*. New York: New American Library, 1977.

Exercise

James F. Fixx, *The Complete Book of Running*. New York: Random House, 1977.

Thaddeus Kostrubala, *The Joy of Running*. Philadelphia: J. B. Lippincott Company, 1976.

Diabetes

June Biermann and Barbara Toohey, *The Diabetes Question and Answer Book.* Nashville, Tenn.: Sherbourne Press, 1972.

A Cookbook for Diabetes. New York: American Diabetic Association, New York.

George F. Schmitt, *Diabetes for Diabetics,* 2d ed. Miami, Fla.: Diabetes Press of America, 1968.

Alcohol

James L. Free, *Just One More.* Palo Alto, Calif.: Bull Publishing, 1977.

Peter M. Miller and Marie A. Mastria, *Alternatives to Alcohol Abuse: A Social Learning Model.* Champaign, Ill.: Research Press, 1977.

GLOSSARY

Acute *(ah-CUTE)*   Indicates illness that appears suddenly or is of short duration.

Angina Pectoris *(AN-jin-ah PEC-tor-us)*   Chest discomfort or pain due to a temporary inadequacy of blood to an area of heart muscle.

Angiocardiography *(AN-jee-oh-kar-dee-OG-rah-fee)*   An x-ray examination of the heart or arteries. Performed by injecting a special dye into the bloodstream, so that the inside of the heart and blood vessels can be seen on either still or moving x-ray film. *See also* Coronary angiography.

Angiogram *(AN-jee-oh-gram)*   The x-ray picture obtained from angiography or angiocardiography.

Angiography *(an-jee-OG-rah-fee)*   X-ray examinations of areas of the body, performed by injecting special dyes. *See* Angiocardiography.

Anoxia *(an-OKS-see-ah)*   Lack or deficiency of oxygen.

Anterior Descending Coronary Artery   The coronary artery that supplies blood to the front wall of the heart. Also called Left Anterior Descending or LAD. *See* Coronary artery.

Anticoagulant *(ant-eye-koh-AG-u-lant)*   Drug that delays blood clotting.

Antihypertensive Agent *(ant-eye-high-per-TEN-siv A-gent)* Drug that lowers blood pressure.

Aorta *(ay-OR-tah)*   Main artery carrying blood from the principal pumping chamber of the heart, the left ventricle, to the other arteries and then to all parts of the body.

Aortic Insufficiency *(ay-OR-tik in-suh-FISH-en-see)*   Improper closing of the valve between the aorta and the lower left chamber of the heart, the left ventricle, thereby permitting a back-flow of blood into the ventricle.

Aortic Stenosis *(ay-OR-tik ste-NOH-sis)*   Narrowing of the aortic valve, the valve between the lower left chamber of the heart, the left ventricle, and the large artery called the aorta. If this narrowing is severe, it places a significant burden on the heart.

Aortic Valve *(ay-OR-tik valv)*   Valve preventing a leakage of blood back from the aorta into the left ventricle.

Aortocoronary Saphenous Vein Bypass *(ay-OR-toh-KOR-oh-na-ree SAH-fe-nus)*   See Coronary bypass.

Arrhythmia *(ah-RITH-mee-ah)*   Abnormal rhythm of the heartbeat, including fast, slow, and irregular rhythms and premature beats.

Arterial Blood *(ar-TE-ree-al)*   Blood carried in the arteries. The blood is bright red because it is rich in oxygen, which it receives in the lungs.

Arteriograms *(ar-TE-ree-oh-grams)*   See Coronary Arteriography, Angiocardiography, Angiogram, and Angiography.

Arterioles *(ar-TE-ree-ols)*   The smallest arterial blood vessels, resulting from repeated branching of the arteries, which carry blood from the arteries to the capillaries.

Arteriosclerosis *(ar-TE-ree-oh-skle-ROH-sis)*   Commonly called "hardening of the arteries." *See also* Atherosclerosis.

Artery *(AR-ter-ee)* Blood vessels that carry blood away from the heart to the various parts of the body.

Atherosclerosis *(ATH-er-oh-skle-ROH-sis)* Narrowing within an artery, consisting of a yellowish material which contains cholesterol, fats, and other debris.

Atrial Fibrillation *(A-tree-al fi-bri-LA-shun)* Rhythm disturbance of the heart in which the atria no longer beat in their typical rhythmic fashion but rather quiver chaotically and ineffectively at extremely rapid rates. This produces an irregular and often rapid rhythm of the main pumping chambers of the heart, the ventricles.

Atrium *(A-tree-um)* One of the two upper receiving chambers of the heart, which collects the blood from the veins and then delivers it to the ventricles. Also termed auricle.

Blood Reddish fluid that flows through the veins and arteries of the body, carrying nutrients to the organs and tissues and carrying wastes to the liver, kidneys, and lungs. It is composed of a liquid called plasma and a series of particles, among which are the red cells that carry oxygen to the tissues, the white cells that fight infection in the body, and the platelets that are involved in the blood clotting process. *See also* Plasma.

Blood Pressure The pressure within the arteries. It is usually described by two numbers. The first is the *systolic pressure* produced when the left ventricle contracts and squeezes the blood out into the arterial system. The second is *diastolic pressure,* that which remains when the left ventricle is resting between beats. Hence, a pressure of 120/80 is read as "120 over 80," the first of the numbers being the systolic pressure and the second being the diastolic pressure.

Blood Vessels The blood vessels consist of three types of branching hollow tubes. The *arteries* carry blood from the heart, branching into smaller and smaller sizes until they become arterioles and then *capillaries,* tiny vessels so small that they can be seen only with a microscope and that form a massive network, delivering the blood to all the cells of the body. After the tissues have received the blood, taking up its oxygen and food and giving up waste products, the blood returns via the *veins,* vessels that have much thinner walls than arteries and that, having collected the blood from all the body, deliver it back into the atria of the heart.

Bradycardia *(brad-ee-KAR-dee-ah)*   Abnormally slow heart rate. Generally less than sixty beats per minute.

Capillaries *(KAP-i-lar-eez)*   Extremely small blood vessels that form networks between arterioles and veins. It is through these vessels that the oxygen and nutrition carried by the blood diffuse to the tissues and organs of the body. *See* Blood vessels.

Cardiac *(KAR-dee-ak)*   Pertaining to the heart.

Cardiac Output   Amount of blood pumped by the heart in a one-minute period.

Cardiologist *(kar-dee-OL-oh-jist)*   Physician specially trained to diagnose and treat heart disease.

Cardiopulmonary Bypass *(KAR-dee-oh-PUL-moh-ner-ee)*   Complex apparatus used during open-heart operations. This machine is connected to the heart and blood vessels and functions both as a pump and as a means of bringing oxygen to the blood, during the time the heart is being operated on, and is either partially or completely nonfunctioning.

Cardiovascular *(KAR-dee-oh-VAS-ku-lar)*   Pertaining to the heart and blood vessels.

Cardioversion *(KAR-dee-oh-VER-shun)*   Correction of a rapid or irregular rhythm disturbance by the application of an electrical shock delivered to the heart through the chest wall.

Catheter *(KATH-e-ter)*   Thin tube inserted into a vein or an artery, usually in the arm or groin, and guided into the chambers of the heart. It is used to take samples of blood, to measure pressures within the heart chambers, and to inject angiographic dye.

Cerebrovascular *(SER-ee-bro-VAS-ku-lar)* Pertaining to the blood vessels in the brain.

Cholesterol *(koh-LES-ter-ol)* Fatlike substance found in many foods, especially meats, shrimp, and egg yolks; it is also manufactured by the body.

Chronic *(KRON-ik)* Used in the field of medicine to describe a disorder present for a prolonged period of time.

Circulation *(ser-ku-LAY-shun)* The course of the blood throughout the body, in effect moving in a circle, from the heart, to the tissues, and then back to the heart.

Circulatory *(SER-ku-lah-to-ree)* Pertaining to the heart, the blood vessels, and the circulation of the blood.

Circumflex Coronary Artery One of the three major coronary arteries. It feeds the left side and part of the back of the heart.

Coagulation *(koh-ag-u-LAY-shun)* Process whereby blood changes from a liquid to a thickened or solid state, as in the formation of a blood clot.

Collateral Vessels (coronary) *(koh-LAT-er-al)* When a coronary artery becomes occluded and can no longer supply an adequate amount of blood to a portion of the heart, the remaining arteries may develop new branches to provide blood to the deficient area. These new branches are termed collateral vessels.

Constriction *(kon-STRIK-shun)* The narrowing of the inside diameter of a blood vessel.

Congestive Heart Failure *(kon-JES-tiv)* *See* Heart failure.

Coronary *(KORE-oh-na-ree)* "A coronary" is another term given for a heart attack. The word technically refers to the heart.

Coronary Angiography *See* Angiocardiography and Coronary arteriography.

Coronary Arteries Arteries that conduct blood to the heart muscle. There are three major coronary arteries. The *right* wraps around the right side of the heart to supply its back side. The *left anterior descending* crosses over the front of the heart. The *circumflex* goes around the left side of the heart. The circumflex and anterior descending branch off from the *left main coronary artery.*

Coronary Arteriogram *(KORE-oh-na-ree ar-TE-ree-oh-gram)* The film or x-ray moving picture that is obtained by coronary arteriography.

Coronary Arteriography *(KORE-oh-na-ree ar-te-ree-OG-rah-fee)* Procedure whereby a special dye is injected into the coronary arteries so that x-ray moving pictures can be taken of the inside walls of these vessels to determine the presence, severity, and location of coronary artery narrowing or occlusion. The procedure is done by threading a small tube through an artery from the groin or arm to a location just above the heart. Dye is also injected into the left ventricle, in an effort to determine whether there has been any temporary or permanent damage to the pumping function of that chamber. *See also* Angiocardiography.

Coronary Bypass Surgery Operation in which a bypass or detour is placed around one or more obstructed coronary arteries, usually by taking a vein (saphenous vein) from the aorta and grafting it to an area of the coronary artery beyond the obstruction, thus permitting a greater supply of blood to the heart.

Coronary Care Unit Area of specialized intensive care in a hospital where patients with suspected or proven heart attacks are initially treated.

Coronary Occlusion *(KORE-oh-na-ree ok-KLU-shun)* Obstruction in one of the branches of the coronary arteries which stops or slows down the flow of blood to some part of the heart muscle.

Coronary Thrombosis *(KORE-oh-na-ree throm-BOH-sis)* Formation of a blood clot in a branch of one of the arteries which conducts blood to the heart muscle. It is a form of coronary occlusion that may lead to a heart attack.

Cor-pulmonale *(kore-pul-mo-NAL-ee)* Heart disease resulting from a disease of the lungs or of the blood vessels in the lungs.

Cyanosis *(sigh-ah-NO-sis)* Blueness of the skin caused by insufficient amount of oxygen in the blood.

Defibrillator *(dee-FI-bre-la-tor)* Machine that delivers an electrical shock to the patient's chest, with the objective of restoring the normal heart rhythm when there has been a rhythm disturbance.

Diabetes *(dye-ah-BEE-teez)* Also called *diabetes mellitus.* Disease in which the body is unable to use sugar normally, owing to insufficient amounts of a substance called insulin, normally produced by the pancreas. Diabetes may lead to coronary artery disease and heart attack.

Diastole *(dye-AS-toh-lee)* Period of the heart cycle when the ventricles are not contracting but rather are resting between beats, filling up with the blood received by the atria.

Dietitian *(dye-e-TISH-an)* Person skilled in the scientific use of diet in health and disease.

Dilatation *(dil-a-TAY-shun)* Stretching, distension, or enlargement of the heart or blood vessels.

Diuresis *(dye-u-REE-sis)* Increased outflow of urine.

Diuretic *(dye-u-RET-ik)* Medication given to increase the amount of urine, utilized to remove excess salt and water from the body.

Dyspnea *(DISP-nee-ah)* Difficult or labored breathing, shortness of breath.

ECG *See* Electrocardiogram.

Edema *(e-DEE-mah)* Swelling, usually of the legs, occasionally of the arms or face, caused by presence of abnormally large amounts of fluid in the tissues of the body.

EKG *See* Electrocardiogram.

Electrocardiogram *(e-LEK-troh-KAR-dee-oh-gram)* Graphic record produced by the electrical voltage changes generated by the heart as it contracts and relaxes. Also called ECG or EKG.

Electrocardiograph *(e-LEK-troh-KAR-dee-oh-graf)* Instrument that records the electrical changes produced by the heart.

Embolus *(EM-boh-lus)* Blood clot or other substance that dislodges from the heart or a blood vessel and travels to and obstructs an artery located downstream. This event is termed an *embolism.*

Endocarditis *(en-doh-kar-DYE-tis)* Infection of the heart valves.

Exercise Test Test of the heart's capacity to function and capacity of the coronary arteries to deliver a sufficient supply of blood to the heart during the work of exercise. This test is usually performed using a motor-driven treadmill or stationary bicycle, and changes in blood pressure, heart rate, and electrocardiogram are recorded. Abnormalities of one of these frequently develop when narrowing of the coronary arteries prevents an adequate supply of blood to the heart during exercise, a period when the needs of the heart are at their greatest.

Extrasystole *(eks-trah-SIS-toh-lee)* A contraction of the heart that occurs prematurely and interrupts briefly the normal rhythm of the heart. Also termed premature beats or ectopic beats.

Fibrillation *(fi-bri-LAY-shun)* Ventricular fibrillation is one type of cardiac arrest or stopping of the heart, where the ventricles no longer beat but rather quiver in an ineffective manner. The pumping action of the heart is therefore lost. *See* Atrial fibrillation.

Fluoroscope *(FLOO-roh-skope)* X-ray instrument with which the physician can view the silhouette of the patient's organs and body structures that lie deep in the body.

Heart Muscular hollow organ in the chest containing four chambers; the principle pump of the body.

Heart Block Interference in the transmission of electrical impulses within the heart, which can then result in irregular rhythms and slowing of the heartbeat.

Heart Failure Also called *congestive heart failure.* A condition whereby the pumping action of the heart is impaired, so that blood backs up into the lungs or other parts of the body. In addition, there is an inadequate delivery of blood and the nutrition that it carries to the tissues of the body.

Heart-Lung Machine Machine through which the body's blood may be detoured in order to dispose of wastes and to acquire oxygen while the heart is opened for surgery. *See* Cardiopulmonary bypass.

Hemiplegia *(hem-ee-PLEE-jee-ah)* Paralysis of one side of the body caused by damage to the opposite side of the brain.

Hemoglobin *(HE-moh-gloh-bin)* Oxygen-carrying red pigment contained in the red blood cells.

Hemorrhage *(HEM-or-ij)* Loss of blood from a blood vessel. In internal hemorrhage, the blood passes into the tissues surrounding the ruptured blood vessel. In external hemorrhage, as in a cut on the skin, it is a bleeding to the outside of the body.

Hypertension *(high-per-TEN-shun)* Commonly called "high blood pressure." An elevation of blood pressure above normal ranges (above 150/90).

Hypercholesterolemia *(high-per-koh-LES-ter-ol-E-me-ah)* Elevation in the amount of cholesterol present in the blood.

Hypotension *(high-poh-TEN-shun)*   Low blood pressure; blood pressure below the normal range.

Infarct *(IN-farkt)*   Area of tissue that is damaged or dies as a result of having received an insufficient supply of blood. Frequently used in the phrase "myocardial infarct," referring to an area of the heart muscle that is damaged because of an insufficient flow of blood through the coronary arteries that normally had supplied it.

Ischemia *(is-KEE-mee-ah)*   A local, usually temporary, lack of blood supply to some part of the body. Often it is caused by a constriction or an obstruction in the blood vessels supplying that area.

Left Main Coronary Artery   Important coronary artery, originating from the aorta, which divides into two other major coronary arteries, the left anterior descending and circumflex coronary arteries.

Left Ventricle   Main pumping chamber of the heart.

Lipid *(LIP-id)*   Fat or fatlike substance. Two of the major lipids implicated in the cause of coronary artery disease are cholesterol and (perhaps less importantly) triglycerides. *See* Cholesterol, Triglycerides.

Malignant Hypertension *(mah-LIG-nant high-per-TEN-shun)*   Very severe high blood pressure, causing rapid damage to the kidney, heart, brain, and other organs.

Mitral Valve *(MYE-tral)*   Valve preventing backflow from the left ventricle to the left atrium.

Murmur   Swishing or blowing sound in the heart, which usually is heard with the aid of a stethoscope and which may be either a normal finding or indicate some type of heart or valve disorder.

Myocardial Infarction *(mye-oh-KAR-dee-al in-FARK-shun)*   Damaging of an area of the heart muscle, resulting from a reduction in the supply of blood reaching that area.

Pacemaker *(PACE-make-er)* Small mass of specialized cells located in the upper right chamber of the heart that creates the electrical impulses that cause the heart muscle to contract in a normal rhythmic fashion. The *artificial* electrical cardiac pacemaker is a device used to substitute for the heart's natural pacemaker, to speed the heartbeat by a series of rhythmic electrical impulses when the heart's own rhythm beats too slowly, as in the instance of heart block.

Palpitation *(pal-pi-TAY-shun)* Sensation of a fluttering, racing, or skipping of the heart noted by the patient.

Pericarditis *(per-i-kar-DYE-tis)* Inflammation or irritation of the pericardium. Pericarditis may have many causes, one being a myocardial infarction.

Pericardium *(per-i-KAR-dee-um)* Thin sac that surrounds the heart.

Phlebitis *(fle-BYE-tis)* Also called *thrombophlebitis.* Inflammation of a vein, usually in a leg. Sometimes a blood clot forms in the inflamed vein and subsequently is carried to a lung, where it becomes an obstruction termed a pulmonary embolus.

Plasma *(PLAZ-mah)* Liquid part of the blood left when the other elements, the red and white blood cells, are removed.

Polyunsaturated Fat *(pol-ee-un-SAT-u-rat-ed)* Fats that are usually liquid oils of vegetable origins. A diet with a high polyunsaturated-fat content tends to lower the amount of cholesterol in the blood slightly.

Premature Beats *See* Extrasystole.

Prophylaxis *(proh-fi-LAK-sis)* Some form of preventive treatment.

Pulmonary Artery *(PUL-moh-ner-ee)* Large artery that carries blood, low in oxygen, from the right ventricle to the lungs.

Pulmonary Edema *(PUL-moh-ner-ee e-DEE-mah)* When congestive heart failure is severe, the fluid within the left heart backs up into the lungs, seeping into the tiny air sacs in the lung, producing severe and oftentimes sudden shortness of breath.

Pulmonary Veins   Four veins that carry oxygen-rich blood from the lungs into the left upper chamber of the heart, the left atrium.

Pulse *(puls)*   Expansion of an artery that results from the pumping of blood by the heart, which may be felt with the fingers when they are placed over an artery.

Regurgitation *(ree-gur-ji-TAY-shun)*   Backward flow of blood through a defective valve in the heart.

Rehabilitation *(re-hah-bil-i-TAY-shun)*   Return of a person disabled by disease or accident to the maximum attainable physical, mental, emotional, social, and economic usefulness.

Rheumatic Heart Disease *(roo-MAT-ik)*   Damage done to the heart, particularly the heart valves, as the result of one or more attacks of rheumatic fever.

Right Coronary Artery   One of three major coronary arteries. It passes across the right side of the heart, then to the back of the heart, where it provides its major blood supply.

Right Ventricle   The pumping chamber of the heart which sends blood into the lungs, so that the blood may take up oxygen.

Saturated Fat *(SAT-u-rate-ed)*   Fats most often of animal origin, such as those contained in milk, butter, and meats, which are usually solid at room temperature. They may raise the blood cholesterol.

Serum *(SIR-rum)*   Liquid part of the blood remaining after it is clotted; the red cells, white cells, and platelets have therefore been removed.

Sphygmomanometer *(sfig-moh-mah-NOM-e-ter)*   Instrument consisting of an arm cuff and a measuring device used to record the blood pressure.

Stethoscope *(STETH-oh-skope)*   Instrument that amplifies the sounds within the body, usually employed by doctors and nurses to listen to a patient's heart and lungs.

Stress Test *See* Exercise test.

Stroke Lack of blood supply to some part of the brain, producing a weakness or paralysis in one or more limbs or a defect in speech.

Symptom *(SIMP-tum)* Description by a patient of his own medical problem.

Syncope *(SIN-koh-pee)* Fainting.

Systole *(SIS-toh-lee)* Period when the heart muscle contracts.

Target Heart Rate Desired heart rate to be attained during an exercise conditioning program.

Tachycardia *(tak-ee-KAR-dee-ah)* Abnormally fast heart rate. Generally, a rate of over 100 beats per minute.

Therapist *(THER-ah-pist)* Person skilled in the treatment of disease or disability.

Thrombophlebitis *See* Phlebitis.

Thrombosis *(throm-BOH-sis)* Formation or presence of a blood clot inside a blood vessel or a cavity of the heart.

Thrombus *(THROM-bus)* Blood clot that forms inside of a blood vessel or in the cavity of the heart.

Treadmill Test *See* Exercise test.

Triglyceride *(try-GLIS-er-ide)* One type of fat or lipid, present in the blood and body tissues. Triglycerides have been considered to be important in the development of coronary artery disease, although evidence for this is less sound than that for cholesterol.

Vasodilator *(vas-oh-DYE-late-or)* Any substance or drug that causes the muscles of the arteries to relax, dilating or widening the hollow passageway within these tubular structures.

Vasopressor *(vas-oh-PRES-or)* Any agent or drug that causes the muscles of the arteries to contract, constricting the arteries and often raising the blood pressure.

Vein *(vane)*   Blood vessel that carries blood from the various parts of the body back to the heart.

Vena Cava *(VEE-nah KAY-vah)*   One of two large veins returning blood from the upper and lower parts of the body to the right upper chamber of the heart, the right atrium.

Venous Blood *(VEE-nus)*   Blood returning from the tissues, which has given up its oxygen and therefore is a more purplish or bluish color.

Ventricles *(VEN-tri-kels)*   The major pumping chambers of the heart. *See* Left ventricle and Right ventricle.

APPENDIXES

Further Explorations

APPENDIX A

Common Cardiovascular Drugs: Detailed Notes

THIS appendix describes details about the most commonly used cardiovascular drugs. If your doctor puts you on any medicines, be sure to check to see if they are discussed. If not, there is a blank *Personal Drug Information Sheet* on page 187. Ask your doctor or nurse to fill it out for you.

The drugs discussed below, categorized according to how they work, are drugs that:

- Lower blood pressure.
- Remove excess water from the body.
- Resupply the body with necessary potassium.
- Correct irregular heart rhythms.
- Increase the pumping action of the heart.
- Prevent and treat angina pectoris.
- Lower blood-fat content.
- Slow down clotting of the blood.

Drugs that Lower Blood Pressure (Antihypertensives)

SCIENTIFIC NAMES:	*Alpha-methyl-dopa, Reserpine, Guanethidine, Clonidine*
TRADE NAMES:	*Aldomet, Ismelin, Catapres, Serpasil*
Form:	Tablet
Administration:	Orally
Action and Uses:	Reduce blood pressure by indirectly relaxing the muscular walls of the blood vessels
Possible Side Effects:	Variable, but may include: Drowsiness Depression Dizziness or fainting (especially when one stands up suddenly) Fatigue Difficulty sleeping Nasal stuffiness Change in sexual potency
Special Instructions:	The sudden discontinuation of Catapres may produce a severe rise in blood pressure and is therefore to be avoided.
SCIENTIFIC NAMES:	*Hydralazine, Prazosin*
TRADE NAMES:	*Apresoline, Minipress*
Form:	Tablet
Administration:	Orally
Action and Uses:	Lower blood pressure by directly relaxing the blood vessels
Possible Side Effects:	Dizziness Fainting (especially when one stands up suddenly) Sensation of flushing of the skin

DIURETICS	Diuretics are discussed in detail on page 178.
Action and Uses:	Lower blood pressure by increasing the outflow of salt and water by the kidneys, which decreases the amount of fluid present in the bloodstream, decompresses the system, and lets pressure in the blood vessels fall. Also relax the walls of the vessels and thereby reduce the blood pressure.
PROPRANOLOL	Propranolol is discussed in detail on page 181.
Action and Uses:	Lowers blood pressure in two principal ways:

1. The amount of blood ejected by the heart with each beat is reduced so that the blood pressure within the arteries falls.
2. It inhibits, in a very complicated way, the constriction of arteries and therefore allows them to relax, with a consequent drop in blood pressure.

"COMBINATION DRUGS"	
Form:	Tablets that contain drugs from two or three of the categories listed above.
TRADE NAMES:	*Aldoril, Aldactazide, Diupres, Renese-R, Salutensin, and Ser-Ap-Es*

Drugs that Remove Excess Water from the Body (Diuretics or "Water Pills")

SCIENTIFIC NAMES: *Hydrochlorothiazide, Chlorothiazide, Furosemide, Ethacrinic Acid, Many Others*

TRADE NAMES: *Hydrodiuril, Diuril, Lasix, Edecrin, Dyazide, Enduron, Naqua, Naturetin, Renese, Aldactone, Dyrenium, Aldactazide, Regroton*

Form: Tablet

Administration: Orally

Action and Uses: Remove excess amounts of water and salt from the body by causing increases in the amount of urination. Often used for this purpose in congestive heart failure. Also used to lower blood pressure of some patients.

Possible Side Effects:
1. Loss of the mineral potassium from the body can occur with most diuretics, but seldom with Dyazide, Dyrenium, Aldactone, or Aldactazide. Your physician may order a blood test to check your potassium from time to time.
2. Muscle cramps
   Muscle weakness
   Loss of appetite
   Symptoms of gout

Special Instructions:
1. One of the liquid potassium preparations or foods rich in potassium are often used in conjunction with some of the diuretics to prevent the excessive loss of potassium from the body. This is especially important when

one of the digitalis preparations
also is being taken.
2. It is a good idea to weigh yourself
daily, in the morning, to check the
amount of water loss.

Drugs that Resupply the Body with Necessary Potassium

SCIENTIFIC NAME:	*Potassium*
TRADE NAMES:	*Potassium Chloride, K-Lyte, Slow-K, Kato, K-Lor, Kay-Ciel, Many Others*
Form:	Usually a liquid. Also comes as a powder that can be dissolved in water or juice. Occasionally pills are given.
Administration:	Orally
Action and Uses:	Resupply the body with the potassium it may have lost as the result of the action of a diuretic.
Possible Side Effects:	Gastrointestinal distress including nausea, vomiting, or diarrhea Loss of appetite Abdominal burning
Special Instructions:	1. Potassium is also found in many foods: oranges, melon, dried fruit, potatoes, pineapple, tomatoes, grapefruit, prunes, bananas, apricots, cabbage, raisins, cantaloupe, meats, poultry, or fish. These can be used as supplemental sources of potassium. 2. The medication often tastes bad and causes stomach upset. Taking it with fruit juice or changing brands of potassium may be helpful.

Drugs that Correct Irregular Heart Rhythms (Antiarrhythmics)

SCIENTIFIC NAMES:	*Quinidine*
TRADE NAMES:	*Quinidine, Quinaglute, Cardioquin*
Form:	Tablet
Administration:	Orally
Action and Uses:	Correct irregular heart rhythm, premature beats, and some types of very rapid heart action (tachycardias)
Possible Side Effects:	Gastrointestinal discomfort, including nausea, vomiting, or diarrhea Loss of appetite Ringing in ears
Special Instructions:	If you develop small or large bruises or have fainting spells, *contact your physician immediately.*
SCIENTIFIC NAME:	*Procainamide*
TRADE NAME:	*Pronestyl*
Form:	Capsule
Administration:	Orally
Action and Uses:	Correct irregular heart rhythm, premature beats, and some types of very fast heart rates (some tachycardias)
Possible Side Effects:	Gastrointestinal distress, including nausea, vomiting, or diarrhea Fever Skin rash Aching joints Dizziness

Special Instructions:	It may be necessary to take this drug every 3 to 6 hours for it to be effective. Ask your physician. Check with your doctor if you develop arthritis or aching joints.
SCIENTIFIC NAME:	*Disopyramide*
TRADE NAME:	*Norpace*
Form:	Capsule
Administration:	Orally
Action and Uses:	To correct irregular heart rhythm, premature beats, and some types of very fast heart rates (some tachycardias)
Possible Side Effects:	Dry mouth Constipation Difficulty with urination Dryness of eyes, nose and throat Loss of appetite Gas bloating Nervousness Fatigue Edema or weight gain
Special Instructions:	Call physician if fainting or severe dizziness occurs.
SCIENTIFIC NAME:	*Propranolol*
TRADE NAME:	*Inderal*
Form:	Tablet
Administration:	Orally
Action and Uses:	Prevents and treats fast or irregular heartbeats, lowers blood pressure, prevents pain of angina pectoris.
Possible Side Effects:	Gastrointestinal distress, including nausea, vomiting, or diarrhea

Fatigue, sleepiness, difficulty
    sleeping, mental slowing
Shortness of breath
Wheezing
Slowing of heart rate to less than
    50 beats per minute
Increase in body weight owing to
    retention of body fluids

Special Instructions: Your physician should be advised if
you have shortness of breath, gain
more than 4 pounds in a few days or
detect an undue slowing of your
heart rate. Some patients who have
asthma or diabetes may have other
side effects that can be discussed
with a physician. This medication
should not be stopped abruptly
without advice from a physician if
you have angina pectoris.

Drugs that Increase Pumping Action of the Heart

SCIENTIFIC NAMES: *Digitalis, Digoxin, Digitoxin*

TRADE NAMES: *Lanoxin, Crystodigin*

Form: Tablet

Administration: Orally

Action and Uses: Increase the pumping strength of the
heart in cases of congestive heart
failure. Also, correct some forms of
irregular or rapid heartbeats.

Possible Side Effects: Gastrointestinal distress,
    including nausea, vomiting, or
    diarrhea
Visual disturbances
Heart palpitations

Skipped or premature beats
Slowing of heart rate

Special Instructions:

1. If any of the above symptoms occur or if your heart rate drops below 50 beats per minute, *contact your physician.*
2. If you are taking water pills (diuretics), you may have an increased sensitivity to some of these side effects. If you are taking a digitalis preparation and a diuretic, your physician may have you take potassium to help avoid these side effects.

Drugs that Help Prevent and Treat Angina Pectoris (Antianginals)

SCIENTIFIC NAMES:
Nitroglycerin, Glycerine Trinitrate

TRADE NAMES:
Nitro-Bid, Nitrol, Nitrospan, Nitrostat, Nitrone

Form:
Tablet or paste

Administration:
Held under the tongue or rubbed on the skin

Action and Uses:
Prevent and treat angina pectoris

Possible Side Effects:
Headache or fullness in the head
Flushing of the skin
Dizziness and fainting (especially upon standing suddenly)

Special Instructions:
These tablets must be kept in a well-sealed dark container supplied by your pharmacist or they will lose their potency in about six months.

SCIENTIFIC NAMES:	*Isosorbide Dinitrate*
TRADE NAMES:	*Isordil, Sorbitrate*
Form:	Tablet and capsule
Administration:	Swallowed or held under the tongue
Action and Uses:	Prevent and treat angina pectoris and, more recently, treat heart failure
Possible Side Effects:	Headache or fullness in the head Flushing of the skin Dizziness (especially when one stands up suddenly) Fainting
Special Instructions:	If fainting occurs, your physician should be advised.

Drugs that Help Lower Blood-Fat Levels (Lipid-Lowering Drugs)

SCIENTIFIC NAME:	*Clofibrate*
TRADE NAME:	*Atromid-S*
Form:	Capsule
Administration:	Orally
Action and Uses:	Lowers high levels of triglycerides and, in some cases, lowers high levels of cholesterol
Possible Side Effects:	Nausea Loss of appetite Aching muscles Atromid-S may add to the effect of anticoagulants such as Coumadin, increasing the risk of bleeding

SCIENTIFIC NAMES:	*Cholestyramine, Colestipol*
TRADE NAMES:	*Questran, Colestid*
Form:	Powder
Administration:	Orally, dissolved in juice, beverage, applesauce, and so on.
Action and Uses:	Lowers the blood cholesterol
Possible Side Effects:	Constipation Abdominal discomfort Nausea Deficiencies in certain vitamins may occur (vitamins A, D, K), which may lead to bleeding tendencies. These are avoided by taking vitamin supplements under your physician's supervision.
Special Instructions:	Always mix with a liquid or semiliquid food. Use in conjunction with a low-cholesterol, low-fat diet. This drug may interfere with the actions of other medications, so that you should always check with your physician when taking other drugs.

Drugs that Slow Down Clotting of Blood (Anticoagulants)

SCIENTIFIC NAMES:	*Warfarin, Dicumarol*
TRADE NAME:	*Coumadin*
Form:	Tablet
Administration:	Orally
Action and Uses:	Slows down the clotting action in the blood to prevent the development of a blood clot or thrombus in an artery or a vein.

Possible Side Effects: Bleeding: red urine, red or black bowel movement, excessive bleeding when cut, nose bleeds, bleeding gums
Appearance of black and blue marks on the skin

Special Instructions: If any of the above symptoms occur, contact your physician. A blood test called prothrombin time or Pro-time must be taken periodically to ensure that the correct amount of the drug is being taken. Many drugs such as aspirin, arthritis medications, sleeping pills, and antibiotics may interact with this drug, changing its potency and its effect. Check with your physician before taking any other medications.

Drugs that May Lessen Seriousness of a New Heart Attack

Can any medication lessen the seriousness of another heart attack, should one come along? There have been several clinical studies suggesting the possibility that one or another drug might just have such a desirable effect.

Drugs currently being looked at by medical scientists include sulfinpyrazone (Anturane), dipyridamole (Persantine), aspirin, clofibrate (Atromid), and propranolol (Inderal) or drugs similar to propranolol available in other countries. Whether these drugs in fact work to lessen the likelihood of another heart attack occurring, or reduce its severity is still unproven, nor are we sure how these drugs would work. All have the capacity of acting as a lubricant, making the blood less "sticky," less likely to thrombose. Clofibrate also helps lower the blood triglycerides, and propranolol may prevent serious rhythm disturbances from occurring.

Scientists are actively looking into all of these possibilities, and at the moment there is no definitive answer to this important question. If you have been put on one of these drugs, fine. If not, that's O.K., too, since many physicians hesitate to use a medication until its benefits become clearly known.

Personal Drug Information Sheet

Ask your physician or nurse to fill this out for any drugs prescribed for you that are not discussed in this appendix.

Drug No. 1

SCIENTIFIC NAME:

TRADE NAME:

Form:

Administration:

Action and Uses:

Special Instructions:

Drug No. 2

SCIENTIFIC NAME:

TRADE NAME:

Form:

Administration:

Action and Uses:

Special Instructions:

APPENDIX B

Four Food Groups You Should Eat Every Day

THIS table lists the four food groups that should be eaten most days in order to achieve a balanced diet. It shows the amount of food in each group necessary to provide a nutritious, balanced diet, providing all essential vitamins, minerals, proteins, carbohydrates, and necessary fats.

FOOD GROUP	CONTAINS	SUGGESTIONS FOR A SINGLE SERVING	SERVINGS PER DAY
1. Meat, poultry, fish	Proteins, vitamins, minerals, fats, iron	4 oz. of fish, poultry, or lean meat. Substitutes: natural peanut butter, beans (kidney, lima, baked), split peas.	1
2. Vegetables and fruits	Vitamins, minerals, roughage	½ cup juice, 1 piece fruit, 1 cup vegetables	4
3. Breads and cereals	Proteins, vitamins, minerals, starches, bulk	1 slice bread, 1 cup flaked cereal, ½–⅔ cup cooked cereal	4
4. Dairy	Proteins, vitamins, minerals	1 glass nonfat milk, low-cholesterol cheese, cottage cheese	2

APPENDIX C

Rearranging Your Menu

WHAT YOU USED TO EAT ON A TYPICAL DAY	WHAT YOU CAN EAT TODAY
Breakfast	
Orange juice	Orange juice
Cornflakes with fruit and milk	Cornflakes with fresh fruit and nonfat milk
Scrambled eggs	Scrambled low-cholesterol egg substitute
Sausage	Low-cholesterol sausage substitute
Toast and butter	Toast and corn-oil margarine (or a similar polyunsaturated margarine)
Milk	Nonfat milk
Coffee or tea with cream	Coffee or tea with nondairy creamer
Lunch	
Minestrone soup	Minestrone soup
Baked halibut with lemon	Baked halibut with lemon
Cottage cheese	Low-fat cottage cheese
Sliced zucchini	Sliced zucchini
Fresh fruit	Fresh fruit
Bread and butter	Bread and corn-oil margarine
Coffee or tea with cream	Coffee or tea with nondairy creamer

191

WHAT YOU USED TO EAT ON A TYPICAL DAY	WHAT YOU CAN EAT TODAY
Dinner	
Tomato juice	Tomato juice
Green salad with dressing	Green salad with low-fat dressing
Chicken	Roast chicken (skinned)
Mashed potatoes with butter	Mashed potatoes made with nonfat milk and corn-oil margarine
Green beans	Green beans
French bread and butter	French bread with corn-oil margarine
Pudding	Pudding made with nonfat milk
Wine, milk, or coffee	Wine, nonfat milk, or coffee

APPENDIX D

Shopping Suggestions: How to Read Food Labels

ALL packaged food processors are required to identify the ingredients in their products. By using your knowledge of calories, fats, and cholesterol, you may select for use only those food products that will help provide good nutrition without risk. For example:

Angel Food Cake Mix

INGREDIENTS: Sugar and dextrose, cake flour (bleached), dried egg whites, wheat starch, leavening, tristearin, artificial flavoring.

COMMENT: Looks good.

Black Forest Cake—Prepared and Ready-to-bake

INGREDIENTS: Cherries, sugar, modified whey, corn syrup, enriched flour, fresh whole milk, fresh whole eggs, vegetable shortening, heavy whipping cream, Grade AA butter, chocolate, cocoa, mono- and diglycerides, baking powder, modified food starch, vegetable gum, vanilla, salt, gelatin, ascorbic acid, skim milk, lecithin, vegetable color.

COMMENT: *Caution*—note the milk, cream, eggs, shortening, butter, and chocolate.

Buttermilk Biscuits (Refrigerated)

INGREDIENTS: Enriched bleached flour, water, beef fat, dextrose, hydrogenated vegetable oil, baking soda, salt, corn starch, artificial flavoring.

COMMENT: *Caution*—watch the hydrogenated oil and beef fat.

Mayonnaise (Imitation)

INGREDIENTS: Water, soybean oil, vinegar, egg yolk, modified food starch, salt, mustard flour, xanthan gum, sodium benzoate, preservatives, spices, natural flavor, artificial color.

COMMENT: *Caution*—contains egg yolks, but less than in regular mayonnaise. Regular mayonnaise contains eggs but is acceptable when used in moderation because the amount of egg is small.

Minestrone Soup (Canned)

INGREDIENTS: Beef stock, carrots, potatoes, water, celery, beans, zucchini, salt, potato starch, hydrolyzed plant protein, cheddar cheese and natural flavoring.

COMMENT: The ingredients basically are good.

Pancake Mix (Refrigerated)

INGREDIENTS: Skim milk, enriched bromated flour, liquid sugar, pasturized whole eggs, margarine, corn syrup, buttermilk solids, baking powder, salt, whey solids, vegetable gum, ascorbic acid, artificial coloring.

COMMENT: *Caution*—this batter contains eggs.

Peanut Butter

INGREDIENTS: Peanuts, dextrose, hardened vegetable oils, sugar.

COMMENT: *Caution*—the hardened vegetable oils are heavy in saturated fat content.

Peanut Butter, Natural

INGREDIENTS: Peanuts

COMMENT: This is O.K.

Pudding Mix (Powdered)

INGREDIENTS: Sugar, dextrose, cornstarch, modified cornstarch, salt, vegetable gum, artificial flavor, natural flavor, artificial color.

COMMENT: *Caution*—the content of sugar may be high, and this may be undesirable if you are overweight or have high triglycerides. Pudding made with whole milk is, of course, high in saturated fat.

Tomato Catsup

INGREDIENTS: Tomatoes, sugar, corn syrups, vinegar, salt, dehydrated onion, garlic, spices, and flavoring.

COMMENT: Looks good.

Of course, if you're on a low-salt diet, you should watch for this on the labels, too.

APPENDIX E

Foods Low in Cholesterol and Saturated Fats

SOME commercially available food products that are low in cholesterol and saturated fat are listed below. Many of these will satisfy that sweet tooth. The asterisk (*) indicates that they should be prepared with nonfat milk.

Bacon Substitute

Bac-Os (General Mills)—use in moderation

Cakes

Baker Boy Diet Cake
Holland Honey Cake (Holland Honey Cake Co.)

Cheeses

Cheezola (Fischer Cheese Co.)
Count Down (Fischer Cheese Co.)
Lite-Line (Borden)—use in moderation

Cookies

Almond Paste (El Red)
Barley Fruit (El Molino)
Fruit Bars (El Molino)
Oatmeal and Molasses (El Molino)

Egg Substitutes

Second Nature (Avocet)
Powdered Egg White (Hermingsen Foods, Inc.)—for cooked foods
Egg Beaters (Standard Brands, Inc.)
Scramblers (Morning Star Farms)

Fish

Monarch Dietetic Fish
Mrs. Paul's Fried Fish Fillet
Chicken of the Sea (Dietetic Pack)
White Star Tuna (Dietetic Pack)

Frosting Mixes

Fluffy White (Betty Crocker)
Lemon Fluff (Betty Crocker)
Fresh Vanilla (Betty Crocker)
Fluffy Orange (Pillsbury)
Fluffy Pink (Pillsbury)
Creamy White (Swell)

Ice Cream Toppings

Ice Cream Topping (Towne Pride)
Pineapple, Strawberry (Smuckers)
Marshmallow Creme (Hip-o-lite)
Frozen Fruit Topping (Mariani)

Iced Desserts

Ice milk, all flavors
Strawberry Freeze (Borden)
Imitation Ice Cream (Hi-Saff)
Water Ices
Low-fat frozen yoghurt, all flavors

Margarines

(Margarine in tubs is better than in cubes)
Saffola
Chiffon safflower oil margarine
Fleischmann's
Parkay

Meat Substitutes

Bounty Beef Stew
Morningstar Farm Breakfast Links
Morningstar Farm Sausage
Cellu Ham

Pie Fillings

Chiffon, strawberry, lemon (Jell-O)
Butterscotch (Jell-O)*
Vanilla (Royal)*

Poultry

Lynden Canned Poultry
Swanson Canned Poultry
Bounty Chicken Stew

Puddings

Custard Style Dessert (Royal)*
Danish Dessert, strawberry, raspberry, currant (Junket)
Dietary Pudding, butterscotch, vanilla (D-Zerta)*
Dietary Gelatin Dessert (D-Zerta)
Gelatin (Knox)
Gelatin Dessert, strawberry, lemon, cherry, raspberry (Tillie Lewis)
Junket, raspberry, maple, orange, lemon (Junket)
Pudding, butterscotch (Royal)*
Pudding, instant butterscotch (Royal)*
Pudding, instant vanilla (Royal)*
Pudding, vanilla (Royal)*
Pudding and Pie Mix (Jell-O)*
Pudding Dessert, except chocolate (Tillie Lewis)*

Tapiocas

Pudding, tapioca (Jell-O)*
Pudding, vanilla tapioca (Royal)*

Sauces

Spaghetti sauce with mushrooms (Chef Boyardee)
Spaghetti Sauce (Franco American)
Heinz 57 Sauce
Heinz 57 Savory Sauce

Miscellaneous

Cheese Dip Mix (Schilling)—to be made with cottage cheese
Chili Beans Vegetarian (Las Palmas)
Chili-O-Mix (French)
Corn Bread Mix (Albers)
Corn meal (any brand)
Dinner Cuts (Loma Linda)

Dip mixes, chili, toasted onion, garlic (Laura Scudder's, Schilling)—to be made with dry-curd cottage cheese or low-fat yogurt

Flapjack Mix (Albers)*

Hominy Grits (Albers)

Jonson's Tater Topping (Jonson's)

Meat substitutes (Worthington Foods)

Pancake Mix (Lunds Swedish Pancakes)*

Pancake Mix, buckwheat (Aunt Jemima)*

Pancake Mix, buttermilk (Albers, Aunt Jemima, Duncan Hines, Pillsbury)*

Pancake Mix, wild rice (Hiawatha)*

Spaghetti Sauce Mix (French)

Vegeburger (Loma Linda)

Vegetarian Beans (Heinz)

APPENDIX F

Dining Out

Pᴇᴏᴘʟᴇ tend to take extreme positions about the idea of eating out. Either they think it is nearly impossible (in the United States at least) to avoid loading up on cholesterol, saturated fats, and salt in a restaurant or else they think that if you *do* get a cholesterol-free meal, it will be as bland as the Child's Plate. Some people react by simply having the same rich meals when they eat out that they always have.

There is no need for that. Although the amount of cholesterol and saturated fats that you end up with in the fast-food hamburger franchises is often excessive, in most cases, whether you are in a diner or a five-star restaurant, it is rare that there is a lack of acceptable choice in selections—and certainly not in many of the restaurants with ethnic cuisines such as Chinese and Central and Latin American. Another point: remember that when you are eating out, you're often inclined to treat it as a festive celebration and gorge on food and drink. But of course you don't have to.

Here are some foods you can order when you're in a restaurant:

Appetizers and Snacks

Carrots
Celery
Crab cocktail
Fruit cup
Juice, vegetable or fruit
Mushrooms
Nuts
Pickled herring (avoid if on a low-salt diet)
Radishes
Salads (see below)

Salads

Dressings: Use oil and vinegar or any other not made
    with eggs, cream, or cheeses.
Cottage cheese salads
Fruit salads, all kinds
Vegetable salads, all kinds

Soups

Bean
Clam chowder, Coney Island (red kind, not Boston)
Consommé
Gaspacho
Onion
Pea
Avoid soups made with cream such as bisques. Avoid bouillon
    if you're following a low-salt diet.

Entrees

Entrees are best if broiled or roasted. Avoid rich sauces
    and gravies made with fat, cream, or butter.
Beef (choose the leanest cuts)

Chicken
Fish (preferably not deep fried)
Lamb
Shellfish (crab, lobster, scallops, clams, oysters)
Turkey
Veal

Side Dishes

Mushrooms
Potatoes (including sweet potatoes and yams)
Rice
Spaghetti
Vegetables

Desserts

Angel Food cake
Baked apple
Melon and other fruit, canned, fresh, or frozen
Sherberts
Yogurt, low-fat frozen

Beverages

Alcoholic beverages, beer, and wine (in moderation)
Buttermilk, low-fat
Carbonated beverages
Coffee
Fruit juices
Nonfat milk
Powdered cocoa with nonfat milk
Tea

Sandwiches

Bread should not be made from egg. Sandwich may contain margarine, mayonnaise, catsup, or mustard.

Chicken
Fish
Lettuce
Sprouts
Tomato
Tuna or tuna salad
Turkey

Breakfast Foods

Cereals should be served with nonfat milk.
Cooked cereals, such as oatmeal, Cream of Wheat, Cream
   of Rice
Dry cereals such as Puffed Rice, Shredded Wheat,
   Wheaties
Toast or muffin with margarine or jam

APPENDIX G

Caloric Content of Foods

FOOD	PORTION	CALORIES
Beverages, Alcoholic		
Beer	1 cup (8 oz.)	115
Brandy	1 oz.	70
Eggnog	½ cup	335
Highball	1 cup	165
Port, vermouth, muscatel	½ cup	155
Rum	1 jigger (1½ oz.)	140
Whiskey	1 jigger (1½ oz.)	130
Wine, white, rose	½ cup	85–105
Beverages, Nonalcoholic		
Carbonated soft drinks	1 cup (8 oz.)	80
Chocolate milk	1 cup	200
Cocoa	1 cup	175
Coffee, black	1 cup	1
with cream and sugar		
(1 teaspoon each)	1 cup	45
Tea	1 cup	1
Cereals, Cereal Products		
Bread		
Boston, enriched, brown	2 large slices	200
corn or muffins, enriched	2	220
raisin, enriched	2 slices	130
rye, American	2 slices	110

FOOD	PORTION	CALORIES
white, enriched	2 slices	120
whole-wheat	2 slices	110
Bread, rolls, sweet, unenriched	1	320
Cornflakes	1 cup	100
Crackers		
graham	2	60
saltines	2	30
soda	10 oyster	40
Macaroni, cooked	½ cup	70
Noodles, cooked	1 cup	100
Oatflakes, cooked	1 cup	75
Pancakes, wheat	2 cakes	150
Pie	1 slice	300–400
Popcorn, popped	1 cup	60
Pretzels	15 small sticks	15
Rice, cooked	½ cup	75
Spaghetti	1 cup cooked	220
Tapioca, cooked	½ cup	130
Waffles	1 waffle	225
Wheat germ	1 cup	365
Confectionary, Sugar		
Chocolate, sweetened	2½ oz. bar	335
milk	4 oz.	542
plain	4 oz.	471
Chocolate creames	2	110
Fudge	1 piece	120
Honey	1 tablespoon	65
Jams	1 tablespoon	55
Jellies	1 tablespoon	50
Jelly beans	10 pieces	70
Molasses	1 tablespoon	150
Syrup (chiefly corn syrup)	½ cup	427
Sugar, maple	1 tablespoon	55
cane or beet	1 tablespoon	50
Dairy Products, Eggs		
Cheese, cheddar	1″ square	115
cottage	½ cup	100
cream	2 tablespoons	100
limburger	2 tablespoons	100
parmesan	2 tablespoons	110
roquefort	2 tablespoons	105

FOOD	PORTION	CALORIES
Swiss	2 tablespoons	105
Cream, light	1 tablespoon	30
heavy, or whipping	1 tablespoon	50
Eggs, whole	1 medium	75
Egg white, raw	1 medium	15
Egg yolk, raw	1 medium	60
Milk, pasteurized, whole	1 cup	165
buttermilk, cultured	1 cup	80
canned, evaporated,	½ cup	140
unsweetened, condensed,	½ cup	480
sweetened, nonfat	1 cup	80
Goat's milk	½ cup	71
Ice cream	½ cup	150
Fats, Oils		
Butter	1 tablespoon	100
Mayonnaise	1 tablespoon	100
Olive oil	1 tablespoon	125
Peanut butter	1 tablespoon	85
Fruit, Fruit Juices		
Apples	1 sweet	60–90
Apple juice, fresh	1 cup	120
Apple sauce, sweetened	½ cup	80
Apricot	1 medium	18
Avocados	1 fresh	370
Bananas	1 (about 6 in.)	94
Blackberries, fresh	½ cup	40
canned, sweetened	½ cup	85
Blueberries, fresh	½ cup	45
canned, sweetened	½ cup	110
Cantaloupe	½ fresh	40
Cherries, canned, sweetened	½ cup	100
Cranberry sauce	2 tablespoons	60
Dates, dried	5 pitted	100
Fruit cocktail, canned	½ cup	80
Grapes, fresh	½ cup	68
Grape juice	½ cup	75
Grapefruit	½ (4¼″ dia.)	75
Grapefruit juice, fresh	½ cup	45
Lemons	1 fresh, 2″	30
Olives, green	4 medium	40
Oranges, fresh	1 orange, 3″	70
Orange juice, fresh	½ cup	55

FOOD	PORTION	CALORIES
Peaches, fresh	1 medium, 2½''	45
canned, sweetened	2 halves	85
Pears	1 pear, 2½''	95
Pineapple, canned, sweetened	½ cup	100
Pineapple juice, canned	½ cup	60
Plums	1 plum, 2''	30
Prunes, dried, uncooked	4 large	110
Raisins, dried	½ cup	190
Raspberries, fresh	½ cup	50
canned, sweetened	1 cup	100
Strawberries, fresh	10 large	35
frozen, sweetened	½ cup	125
Meat, Poultry (raw unless otherwise stated)		
Bacon, medium fat, cooked	2 strips	100
Beef (medium fat)		
hamburger, cooked	¼ lb.	225
rib roast, cooked	2 slices (lean-fat)	200–400
rump, cooked	2 slices	190
sirloin, cooked	¼ lb. (lean-fat)	200–300
canned, corned	4 oz.	240
liver	1 slice	85
Chicken		
fried	¼ lb.	275
broiled	¼ lb.	218
liver	¼ lb.	85
Ham		
boiled	¼ lb.	300
smoked, cooked	¼ lb.	400
canned, spiced	¼ lb.	290
Lamb (medium fat)		
leg roast, cooked	¼ lb.	270
rib chop, cooked	¼ lb.	140
Pork (see also Bacon and Ham)		
medium fat	¼ lb.	365
loin or chops, cooked	1 chop	265
Turkey, medium fat	¼ lb.	270
Veal, medium fat	¼ lb. (cutlet-roast)	220–360
Venison	¼ lb.	140
Nuts		
Almonds, salted	15 nuts	100
Brazil nuts	5 nuts	100
Cashew nuts, roasted or cooked	10 nuts	200

FOOD	PORTION	CALORIES
Chestnuts	2 large nuts	30
Peanuts, roasted	½ cup	440
Pecans	1 tablespoon	52
Walnuts	2 tablespoons	95
Sea Food (raw unless otherwise stated)		
Clams, long and round	¼ lb.	80
Cod	1 piece	70
Crab, canned or cooked, meat only	½ cup	85
Flounder	¼ lb.	200
Frog legs	3 large	200
Haddock	¼ lb.	200
Halibut	¼ lb.	200
Lobster	1 (¾ lb.)	300
Oysters	5–8 medium	80
Salmon		
Pacific, cooked	¼ lb.	180
canned	½ cup	190
Sardines, canned in oil	5 medium	180
Scallops, fried	5–6 medium	425
Shrimps, canned, drained	10–12 medium	45
Trout	¼ lb. (brook-lake)	210–290
Soup		
Broth	1 cup	25
Bean	1 cup	260
Beef	1 cup	115
with vegetables	1 cup	80
Chicken noodle	1 cup	68
Lentil	1 cup	600
Pea, creamed	1 cup	270
Tomato	1 cup	100
Vegetable	1 cup	90
Vegetables		
Asparagus, canned	½ cup	25
Beans		
kidney	½ cup	90
lima, fresh	½ cup	90
canned	½ cup	95
snap, fresh	1 cup	35
wax, canned	½ cup	20
Beets (beetroots), peeled, fresh	½ cup	35
Broccoli, fresh	½ cup	20

FOOD	PORTION	CALORIES
Brussels sprouts, fresh	½ cup	30
Cabbage, fresh	wedge	25
Carrots, canned	½ cup	30
fresh	1 carrot, 6''	20
Cauliflower, fresh		25
Celery, stalk	2 stalks	17
Corn, fresh	1 ear (w/butter)	90
canned	½ cup	70
Cucumbers	½ cup, 7½''	20
Eggplant, fresh	½ cup	25
Kale, fresh	1 cup	40
Lentils	½ cup	110
Lettuce, headed, fresh	¼ head	15
Mushrooms (field mushrooms)	½ cup	20
Onions	1 onion, 2½''	40
Peas, green, fresh	½ cup	60
canned	½ cup	70
Peppers, green, fresh	1 large	24
Potato chips	7–10	110
Potatoes, raw	1 medium	90
dehydrated	½ cup	93
french fried	20 pieces	275
Radishes, fresh	4 small	10
Rhubarb, fresh	½ cup	10
Spinach, canned	½ cup	25
Sweet potatoes, fresh	1 small	150
candied	1 medium	300
canned	½ cup	120
Tomatoes	1 medium	35
canned	½ cup	25
Tomato catsup	2 tablespoons	40
Tomato juice, canned	½ cup	25
Miscellaneous		
Gelatin, dry, plain	1 tablespoon	35
dessert	½ cup	60
Yeast, compressed baker's	1 cake	10
Salad dressing		
(French-Thousand Island)	1 tablespoon	60–100

Source: B. J. Sharkey, *Physiological Fitness and Weight Control,* p. 118. Copyright 1974 by Mountain Press Publishing Co., Missoula, Mont. Reprinted by permission.

APPENDIX H

Calories Expended in Various Physical Activities

ACTIVITY	CAL/MIN
Standing, light activity	2.6
Washing and dressing	2.6
Washing and shaving	2.6
Driving a car	2.8
Washing clothes	3.1
Walking indoors	3.1
Shining shoes	3.2
Making bed	3.4
Dressing	3.4
Showering	3.4
Driving motorcycle	3.4
Metal working	3.5
House painting	3.5
Cleaning windows	3.7
Carpentry	3.8
Farming chores	3.8
Sweeping floors	3.9
Plastering walls	4.1
Truck and automobile repair	4.2
Ironing clothes	4.2

ACTIVITY	CAL/MIN
Farming, planting, hoeing, raking	4.7
Mixing cement	4.7
Mopping floors	4.9
Repaving roads	5.0
Gardening, weeding	5.6
Stacking lumber	5.8
Stone masonry	6.3
Pick-and-shovel work	6.7
Farming, haying, plowing with horse	6.7
Shoveling (miners)	6.8
Chopping wood	7.5
Gardening, digging	8.6
Walking upstairs	8–15
Pool or Billiards	1.8
Canoeing: 2.5 m.p.h.–4 m.p.h.	3.0–7.0
Volleyball: Recreational–Competitive	3.5–8.0
Golf: Foursome–Twosome	3.7–5.0
Horseshoes	3.8
Baseball (except pitcher)	4.7
Ping pong–Table tennis	4.9–7.0
Calisthenics	5.0
Rowing: Pleasure–Vigorous	5–15
Cycling: 5–15 m.p.h. (10 speed)	5–12
Skating: Recreation–Vigorous	5–15
Archery	5.2
Badminton: Recreational–Competitive	5.2–10
Basketball: Half–Full Court (more for fast break)	6–9
Bowling (while active)	7.0
Tennis: Recreational–Competitive	7–11
Water skiing	8.0
Soccer	9.0
Snowshoeing (2.5 m.p.h.)	9.0
Handball and squash	10.0
Mountain climbing	10.0
Judo and karate	13.0
Football (while active)	13.3
Wrestling	14.4
Skiing:	
Moderate to steep	8–12
Downhill racing	16.5
Cross-country: 3–8 m.p.h.	9–17

ACTIVITY	CAL/MIN
Swimming:	
Pleasure	6.0
Crawl: 25–50 yds/min.	6–12.5
Butterfly: 50 yds/min.	14.0
Backstroke: 25–50 yds/min.	6–12.5
Breaststroke: 25–50 yds/min.	6–12.5
Sidestroke: 40 yds/min.	11.0
Dancing:	
Modern: Moderate–Vigorous	4.2–5.7
Ballroom: Waltz–Rumba	5.7–7.0
Square	7.7
Walking	
Road–Field (3.5 m.p.h.)	5.6–7.0
Snow: Hard–Soft (3.5–2.5 m.p.h.)	10–20
Uphill: 5–10–15% (3.5 m.p.h.)	8–11–15
Downhill: 5–10% (2.5 m.p.h.)	3.6–3.5
15–20% (2.5 m.p.h.)	3.7–4.3
Hiking: 40 lb. pack (3.0 m.p.h.)	6.8
Running	
12 min. mile (5 m.p.h.)	10.0
8 min. mile (7.5 m.p.h.)	15.0
6 min. mile (10 m.p.h.)	20.0
5 min. mile (12 m.p.h.)	25.0

Source: B. J. Sharkey, *Physiological Fitness and Weight Control,* p. 128. Copyright 1974 by Mountain Press Publishing Co., Missoula, Mont. Reprinted by permission.

Energy Values for Various Physical Activities

THE energy values in these tables are expressed in terms of METs. 1 MET is equivalent to the energy consumed by the body when it is at rest.

ENERGY (METS)	BASIC ACTIVITY	WORK ACTIVITY	LEISURE ACTIVITY
1	Bed rest Sitting Talking Eating	Reading	Reading Watching TV Sewing
1–2	Brushing teeth Shaving Washing hands and face Dressing Strolling on level ground	Sweeping floors Ironing or making bed Washing dishes Typing Driving car	Driving auto Model building Walking
2–3	Walking on level ground, 2 m.p.h. Tub bathing	Light housekeeping Cooking Driving truck Using hand tools Auto repair Waxing floors	Fishing Walking on level ground Golf with power cart Boating

ENERGY (METS)	BASIC ACTIVITY	WORK ACTIVITY	LEISURE ACTIVITY
3–4	Shower bathing Brisk walking, 3 m.p.h. Sexual Intercourse	General house-keeping Farm work Assembly-line work Driving large truck	Golf with pull cart Brisk walking Slow bicycling, 6 m.p.h. Light gardening Horseback riding Sailing Bowling
4–5	Calisthenics Walking, 3.5 m.p.h.	Heavy housework Heavy gardening Lifting and carrying 30 lb. objects Home repairs	Tennis, doubles Heavy gardening Moderate bicycling Slow swimming Dancing Golf, carrying clubs
5–6	Quick walking, 4 m.p.h.	Sawing wood Working heavy tools Lifting and carrying 50 lb. objects Light shoveling Mowing lawn	Fast bicycling Ice skating Hiking Softball Square dancing Hunting
6–7	Jogging, 5 m.p.h.	Shoveling snow Chopping wood	Canoeing Tennis, singles Scuba diving Light downhill skiing Waterskiing
7–8	Climbing stairs Light jogging	Moving heavy objects Lifting and carrying 70 lb. objects	Skiing downhill Paddleboard Swimming backstroke Basketball Ice hockey Mountain climbing
8–9		Lifting and carrying 100 lb. objects	Running, 5½ m.p.h. Handball Swimming breast-stroke Cross-country skiing
10 and over			Fast running, 6 m.p.h. Gymnastics Football Snow sledding

APPENDIX J

Health Organizations to Help You

Among the voluntary health and health-oriented associations equipped to offer assistance to the heart-attack patient during recovery are the following. These are the national headquarters. They can help you locate a branch near you. Or check your telephone book.

American Heart Association
7320 Greenville Avenue
Dallas, Texas 75231
Telephone (214) 750-5300

Nationwide YMCA Cardiovascular Health Program
291 Broadway
New York, New York 10007
Telephone (212) 374-2161

American Lung Association
1740 Broadway
New York, New York 10019
Telephone (212) 245-8000

American Cancer Society
777 Third Avenue
New York, New York 10017
Telephone (212) 371-2900

ACKNOWLEDGMENTS

We are indebted to a great many people for their constructive suggestions.

The following critiqued the manuscript in its entirety: Hillel Abel, M.D.; Kanu Chatterjee, M.D.; Melvin Cheitlin, M.D.; Robert DeBusk, M.D.; Jack Edelen, M.D.; James F. Freis, M.D.; William Hancock, M.D.; William Haskell, Ph.D.; Gary Marcus, M.D.; Lani Moskowitz Strom, R.N.; Pate Thomson, M.D.; and Marianna Pieck, R.N.

Sections of the book were reviewed by Joseph Asturias, R.P.T.; Marlene Bonham, R.P.T.; James Brodale; Michael Bunch, Ph.D.; Kathy Bunch; Sherry Cohn; Teresa Grayson, R.N.; Judy Klausenstock; Kathleen Korcuska; Meredith Jacobs, M.A.; Judith K. Jones, M.D.; Ron Lefkowitz; Judith Levine, R.D.; Sandra Ouye, R.D.; Kathy Reid, O.T.; Lisa Rooney, P.T.; Leslie Roose; Ruth Smestad; Susan Tselos; Phyllis Ullman, R.D.; Sherry Volkert, R.N.; Judy Wachs, M.A., L.M.F.C.; Tracey Wells; and Edna Woitte, R.N.

We are also grateful to William Burgower, Senior Medical Editor, and Warren Robert Stone, Vice President, at Addison-Wesley, for having the confidence to contract to publish our manuscript.

Finally, we want to express our greatest appreciation to Brian Williams for his help and expertise in editing and producing the book. His organizational, writing, and phrase-making abilities, we feel, enormously helped to improve the manuscript.

INDEX